to Lou, may all
your Christmases be
perfect! Love from
Carole xx

The Perfect Christmas

The Perfect Christmas

by

Rose Henniker Heaton

author of
"The Perfect Hostess," "The Perfect Schoolgirl," "Dinner with James"

Illustrated by Daphne Jerrold

BURKE'S PEERAGE

Acknowledgments

MY thanks are due to the memory of Mrs. Beeton and the inspiration of Mrs. C. S. Peel; to Messrs. Jackson of Piccadilly for permission to reprint the recipe for Russian Blenie, and to the Empire Marketing Board for their help. To Messrs. Methuen for permission to use a page from "The Perfect Hostess," (The Domestic Staff give a party). To Messrs. Eyre and Spottiswoode for permission to quote the Rules of Rummy from "Sixteen Gambling Games in Twenty Minutes," and to the proprietors of "The Christian World" for permission to quote from "Christmas-Pie."

It has not been possible to trace the source of the riddles, rhymes, catches and games, but to their gifted authors my grateful thanks are extended.

ROSE HENNIKER HEATON.

This edition published in 1984 by
Burke's Peerage Publications Limited,
1 Hay Hill, London W1X 7LF

ISBN 0 85011 043 2

T.G. Scott & Son Ltd promoted the advertising illustrations

Printed and bound in Great Britain
at The Pitman Press, Bath

Contents

The Perfect Christmas

IT is now Christmas, and not a cup of drink must pass without a Carol: the beasts, fish and fowl come to a general execution, and the corn is ground to dust for the bakehouse and the pastry—Now good cheer and welcome, and God be with you.

NICHOLAS BRETON, 1626.

The Right People to Invite

Cheerful people.
Lots of young people.
The guest with a car.
The Enterprising Girl.
The Elderly Woman who can tell fortunes.
The Elderly Man (if red-faced and jolly).
The Handy-Man (issue invitation early, as he is in great demand).
Anybody good with children.
The Unselfish Friend.

The Wrong People to Invite

The Bone-lazy.
The Egoist.
Mischief-makers.
Spoil-sports.
The Greedy and the Selfish.
Mean People (who suffer tortures at Christmas).
People who always feel " out of things." *

* *Note.*—This may seem hard, but such people should be invited in the summer, when the days are long and you have plenty of time.

You Invite your Nice, but Impecunious Country Cousin for Christmas

(1) In your invitation, make it quite clear that you intend paying her railway ticket and incidental expenses.

(2) On receiving her acceptance, send her the money promptly. Don't wait for Christmas Day, but let her have her presents *at once.* The most useful thing you can possibly send her is a black lace evening frock, and the most useless is a gorgeous feather fan. In smaller ways she would like good gloves, or shoes, and she would probably appreciate the money for a permanent wave.

(3) Don't take too much advantage of her terrible good-nature in doing odd jobs.

(4) Give her a gas fire in her bedroom, and a hot-water bottle in her bed.

(5) Theatres mean a lot to country cousins, and she may prefer two cheap seats to one good one.

(6) If you are going to have her at all, do her handsomely !

How to Ruin Christmas

Grumble at everything and everyone.

Moan at the mention of presents.

Scramble wildly at the last moment for people you dislike, rather than be left alone.

Do nothing for anyone, and expect everyone to wait on you.

Eat too much, and drink far too much.

Spend too much, and grumble while spending it.

Spend too little, and grudge even that.

Leave everything to the last, and sit up until 4 a.m. tying up parcels, and decorating madly.

Start a family quarrel.

Some Suggestions for Spoil-Sports

Develop measles on arrival.

Lose your luggage, and spend your time being motored backwards and forwards to the station to fetch it.

Say you cannot eat rich food, and ask for ground-nuts at every meal.

Turn the Wireless on for a Lecture on World Problems, when the others wish to dance.

Monopolise the telephone when the hostess wishes to order food.

Talk incessantly about the " Mahvellous Christmas you had in Switzerland or Cannes or Cairo," and compare it unfavourably with your present surroundings.

Be rude to any old people ; tease any children ; overfeed the dog.

A Word about

Practical Jokes

Practical Jokers should take out a Life Insurance, as there is a strong prejudice in favour of slaughtering them on sight.

However (as some people seem to like them), here is a list of the horrors that went on when Grandpapa was young, and Merry England *was* Merry England :—

(1) Change the luggage labels on the luggage of departing guests.

(2) Bribe the Housemaid to pack only left-hand shoes and gloves.

(3) Remove drawers from chest of drawers ; turn chest upside down, replace drawers, and turn it the right way up again. When opened, everything falls on the floor.

(4) Arrange to have an invisible guest at dinner, and everyone must address remarks to him, and roar at his jokes (" Ah ha, that was a good one ! "), except the one person on whom the trick is being played.

(5) Replace the brown sugar with ginger (a little crude, perhaps).

(6) Dress up as the AcQuot of Biffisland, complete with Interpreter, and drive over to tea with a neighbour.

The Twelve Days of Christmas

On the twelfth day of Christmas my true love sent to me,

Twelve drummers drumming
Eleven pipers piping
Ten lords a-leaping
Nine ladies dancing
Eight maids a-milking
Seven swans a-swimming
Six geese a-laying
Five gold rings:
Four calling birds
Three French hens
Two turtle doves
And a partridge in a pear tree.

How to Enjoy Christmas

Let the Young Folks themselves take a hamper of good food and presents to a family in desperate need.

N.B.—There are other ways of enjoying Christmas, but this is easily the best.

Cards, Calendars and Stockings

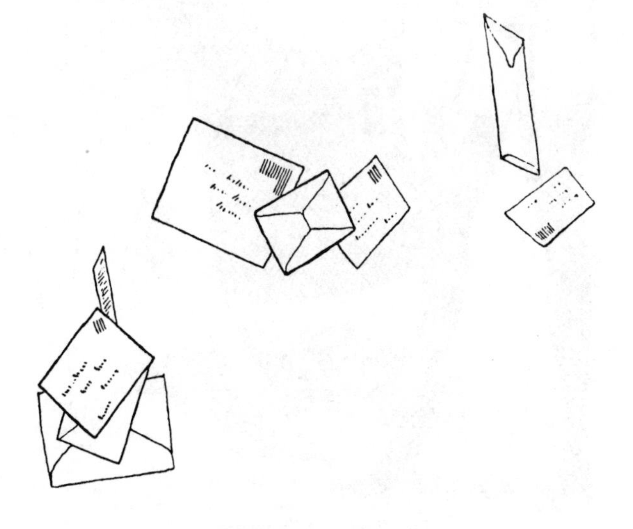

Cards and Their Menace

(1) Never write your name in ink on a card, as the recipient cannot then send it on elsewhere. (Unless, of course, she tears out the inside leaflet.)

(2) A beautiful card is better than a rubbishy present, and at all events it doesn't involve the letter of thanks.

(3) It is a bad, bad plan to use up a last year's card by returning it to the original sender, crossing out "*From* Charles *to* Lottie" and simply substituting "*To* Charles *from* Lottie."

(4) It is as well to read the words on a card, or you may send a new acquaintance a message saying frankly OLD Friends Are Best.

(5) Do not buy one of those misleading cheques—£1,000 worth of Happiness. (Such a blow might easily cause a heart attack or an apoplectic fit.)

What to do with old Christmas Cards. Keep them for a wet day, and then let the children paste them into an album for a hospital.

The Kind of Cards People Really Like

Anything *personal!* A regimental or naval card; an old flower print; a picture of a queer part of the world; dogs really well drawn; gay gardens. High-brows like picture postcards from the National Gallery, and Low-brows like something cheerful. Children like pictures of dogs and kittens and golliwogs, and no one likes a picture of two hands grasping, called " Hands across the Sea," because they have seen it too often.

Calendars People Really Like

(1) Engagement Calendars with a space for every day for a month.

(2) Calendars with the figures printed in gigantic size.

(3) " The Favourite Author " series, if you can find out who it is they particularly admire, and don't send a Dickens calendar to someone who only reads " moderns."

(4) A Gardening Hints Calendar to the gardener.

(5) Genuine Chinese prints on rice-paper. (Very charming.)

(6) A leather pocket Engagement Calendar, with pencil attached, and containing a list of social and racing fixtures.

The Perfect Stocking

A large-size golf stocking. A tangerine (wrapped in gold paper) in the toe and a tinsel ball in the heel help to preserve the shape.

A packet of Alphabet biscuits that spell "A Happy Christmas."

Chocolate letters that spell the owner's name.

A purse with a new sixpence in it.

A box of Dominoes.

Happy Families.

A walnut with either a thimble or toy soldier inside.

Chocolates covered in gold and silver that look like money.

A magnet.

Some wire puzzles.

A pencil sharpener like a globe of the world.

A box of chalks.

A little box of "transfers."

Gay crackers sticking out of the top.

The House-Party

Young gallants and ladies shall foot it along,
Each room in the house to the musick shall throng,
Whilst jolly carouses about they shall pass,
And each country swain trip about with his lass;
Meantime goes the caterer to fetch in the chief,
Plum-pudding, goose, capon, mince pies, and roast-beef.

". . . and this one's from the children!"

Christmas isn't a Perfect Christmas without
Harvey's Bristol Cream.

The House-Party

It is open to question whether people prefer to be left free to amuse themselves, or whether it is advisable to provide a set of amusements for them.

Should the latter be decided on, there is nothing more satisfactory than a Tournament of some form or another.

(1) You might arrange with a neighbouring hostess that *her* guests should meet *your* guests at the Golf Club for a competition.

(2) Arrange a Bridge Tournament.

(3) Arrange a " Games " Tournament one afternoon.

(4) Ping-Pong Tournament.

(5) Treasure Hunt.

(6) Amateur Theatricals.

Little Things that Enliven House-Parties

(1) Cutting a lead pencil in half with a pound note.

A holds a pencil horizontally between both hands. B folds a pound note lengthwise twice. With the sharp edge of the pound note B strikes the pencil smartly, and it breaks.

(2) The Rope Trick.

Get two lengths of rope each about two yards long.

Captain Pink ties loops at each end of his rope and passes his wrists through them.

Major Scarlet passes his rope once through Captain Pink's rope and then gets someone to tie loops at each end of his rope through which he passes his wrists.

Captain Pink and Major Scarlet are now tied together, and their object is to get free.

Some people find that by lying on the floor they do it more easily, and it is certainly more entertaining for the spectators : others try various other contortions, all highly recommended by the onlookers.

Little Tricks for Country Houses

BELIEVE IT OR NOT

If you throw an egg out of a top-storey window on to the lawn it will not break.

If you try to break an egg by squeezing it in your hand, you will not be able to do so.

An Invitation

SUMMONS.

NOTICE TO APPEAR

In re GEORGE HAVALARK / GEORGINA HAVALARK } *v.* MARGOT HITITUP.

In The Above Matter

YOU THE DEFENDANT

ARE HEREBY ORDERED TO APPEAR IN PERSON to show cause why you should not drink

COCKTAILS

&

SHERRY

and eat various Hors d'Œuvres, etc., and meet several other defendants on

DECEMBER 28, 193–

between the hours of 6 p.m. and 7 p.m.

Plaintiffs to this action { GEORGE HAVALARK, GEORGINA HAVALARK.

Kindly hand this Summons to Clerk on arrival.

The Wine and the Walnuts

(With neither Corkscrew nor Nutcrackers.)

(*Kindly supplied by Midshipman Carry-on, R.N.*)

How to open a Bottle of Burgundy without a corkscrew:

Take off your dinner jacket and wrap it carefully round the bottle. You then hit the bottom of the bottle repeatedly and gently against the wall.

The liquid forces the cork gradually up the neck of the bottle, and the only difficulty is to know the exact moment to pull out the cork. Complete mugs sometimes smash the bottle, ruin their dinner jackets and splash the wall-paper.

To crack Walnuts without nutcrackers:

Put the first finger of your left hand on the crack between the shells, and then bring the fist of your right hand smartly down on your left finger, and there you are. Too easy.

A Progressive Dinner-Party

(*This page would make Brillat Savarin turn in his grave. It is intended only for the youthful and unsophisticated.*)

A certain number of motor-cars are necessary.

Neighbours, within a radius of say ten miles, will each provide one course. Let us say there are six couples :—

Mrs. Mountjoy at The Cedars will welcome the guests to Asparagus Soup.

Lady St. Ubbs at The Manor Farm will provide them with salmon and tartare sauce.

Mrs. Hufford at Hufford Hall will expect them to pick at a pheasant.

Colonel Golightly at Box Cottage prides himself on his choice of savouries.

And, finally, they all assemble at Cheviot Lodge for coffee and an impromptu dance.

The Woolworth Party

This is a delightful party, and can be played by any number—young and old.

You choose a wet afternoon when outdoor amusements are impossible, and you present each of your guests with sixpence. They take themselves off to Woolworth's, and each buys secretly what he or she considers the best bargain. After tea these are all spread out in the drawing-room, and there is voting for the Best Bargain. Or each girl can wear her bargain and let the others spot it if they can.

N.B.—When we last played this game, Algernon B. was disqualified for " entering " a grand piano, and saying he had bought it at 3*d*. a note.

The Underground Game

This is a most delightful game for a winter afternoon, and can be played by any number of couples.

Briefly, you plan out a circular tour on the Underground Railway, and rival couples start in opposite directions, and the first couple home wins the game.

This is the game in its crudest form, but the "rules" make for excitement.

(1) Anyone taking a taxi is disqualified.

(2) You must go up at least one moving staircase, and buy a fresh ticket.

(3) You must have a cup of tea at any Lyons you consider least crowded (or the Ritz or Berkeley).

(4) You must buy a packet of cigarettes at one station, and at another station you must buy an evening paper.

(5) You must not cheat.

The Skating Party

Nothing can be more delightful than a Skating Party. Having secured the right temperature, send out invitations by telephone saying everyone is to be expected on the ice at 11 a.m.

Your duty will be to supply wooden benches (from the local school house), a number of rugs, set a brazier burning, and take coffee, cherry brandy and ginger-snaps.

Note.—It is very important not to forget some kind of food. I remember a party where the skaters were provided only with cherry brandy, and although they were curiously successful in cutting eights and grape vines, still the experiment was not considered a success, and could never be repeated.

The Ghost Story Night

For the telling of ghost stories, it is advisable to use the largest room in the house, and have the lights dimly shaded, or merely the flickering firelight. It is as well to begin a story with: " *It happened in a room very like this* "—and you must arrange for one of your friends to open the window quietly when you come to the sentence: " *He* (*or she*) *felt a rush of cold air*." . . . Then it rather improves things if in the middle of a story a stranger comes in, lights a candle and blows it out. Someone will say: " Who was that ? " and you should be able to work it in rather effectively by saying *you saw no one*.

Nothing is more hair-raising than a simple story such as the *Lady's-maid with the Cold Fingers*, and how she always used to come and do up your frock when you were staying in that old house in Scotland. . . . Then there is rather a pleasant thrill about the Butler who always stood behind the chair of anyone who was about to die, and one night you saw him pouring out wine with a fiendish expression into the glass of the Squire. There are some nice ones about a creeper that grows outside the billiard-room, and the tendrils try to come in and strangle any stranger in bed. They wake up screaming, and when the doctor comes, he always finds marks on their throats like a fine cord. Etc., etc.

In fact, you must display an utter disregard for truth, or give up the idea altogether.

THE MOST LURID GHOST STORY

Major Fitz-Alwyn did not believe in ghosts. When he arrived to stay at Maltraver Castle he was put into the Haunted Room. To guard against practical jokers (and his own imagination) he shut and wedged the windows; he damped down the fire to prevent shadows appearing on walls or ceiling; he locked and bolted the door; and finally he blew out the candle, and just as he was preparing to get into bed a sepulchral voice from the pillow said:

NOW WE ARE LOCKED IN FOR THE NIGHT!

THE SHORTEST GHOST STORY IN THE WORLD

"I don't believe in ghosts," said the man in the Club.

"Don't you?" said the man in the chair opposite, and vanished.

A Celebrity Tea

This is excellent where nobody knows anyone else. On arrival, each guest has the name of a celebrity pinned on her or his back. They are allowed to ask other people three questions :

Ex. Am I a man ?
Am I alive ?
Am I a comfort or a curse ?

The other person is allowed to ask three questions in return, and then, armed with such information, they each move on to another victim. The moment they have guessed who they are, they return to the hostess, who pins another name on their back, and off they go again.

The person who has collected most labels by the end of the evening wins the game.

The only " replies " allowed are " Yes," " No," and " I don't know," but it is only fair to say a great deal of helpful cheating goes on in this game (and that's where an extra prize for honesty comes in useful).

Games for the Grown-ups

PEDIGREES: You fix on a mutual friend, and each writes his or her pedigree, which is read aloud :—

Ex. Adolphus Fitznoodle by Royal Enclosure out of Jester.

CHARACTER: You write down a list of virtues, and give your friends marks for them; Maximum 10.

Ex. Beauty.
Charm.
Truthfulness.
Sense of Humour.
Tact.
Sincerity.
Taste.
Common Sense.
Originality.
Generosity.
Good Temper.
Social Gifts.
Etc., etc.

REPRESSIONS: You all make a list of "Six Things I have never had enough of." In a recent newspaper competition the prize was awarded to—

Sun.
Fun.
Sense.
Pence.
Kind words.
Cross words.

(The Runner-up for first prize was "Seeing the owner chasing his hat down the street on a windy day.")

THAT REMINDS ME: You choose a mutual friend, and each write down what he reminds you of. *Ex.*:

Major Rumble Tiger.

A motor-car: A Fire Brigade Lorry.
A song: My Old Shako.
A book: With Rod and Gun.
A bird: Turkey.
An animal: A Rhino.
A town: Kabul.
A drink: Port.
A dish: Curry and Chutney.
A dance: Fandango.

A Games Evening for the Old Folk

(1) Every guest is told to bring a photograph of himself or herself at the earliest possible age. These are all spread round the room and numbered, and a prize is given to the one who guesses the greatest number. There should also be a table set aside for celebrities of a past age, such as Queen Victoria, Mr. Gladstone, Mr. Bright, the Empress Eugenie, Madame Patti, Abraham Lincoln, Lord Tennyson, etc., etc.

(2) SUPPER. INTERVAL

(3) A gramophone record is put on with a medley of old-fashioned tunes, and the audience are invited to write down the names they can remember. The record will be played through twice, and prizes given for the best answers.

The Evening should end with a set of the Lancers to "The Mikado."

A Competition Evening

Plenty of small prizes in preference to one big one. A prize for each event, one for " General Proficiency " and one for " General Inefficiency."

(1) *Dish and Fish :* Each competitor is given a paper fan and a piece of red tissue-paper cut in the shape of a goldfish. At the end of the room are four cardboard (picnic) dishes. The race is run in heats (four people at a time), and the object is to fan the fish into the dish first.

(2) *The Grand Slashional :* This also is run in heats (six at a time). Six pieces of narrow red tape are fastened to one end of the room, and each player is provided with a jockey cap and a pair of curved nail scissors, their object being to cut their piece of tape up the centre. If they cut off a piece of tape, they must begin at the beginning (which is even more difficult, as the tape is narrower). Bookies do a roaring trade with penny and halfpenny coins, and altogether it is a most popular event.

(3) *The Problem Picture :* You must cut out three rather striking but ambiguous magazine pictures, and pin them up on the wall. The guests are required to write on a postcard the most ingenuous explanation of the picture.

SIX OLD AND TRIED FAVOURITES

(1) Pin well-known advertisements on the wall, and make the guests guess the article they represent.

(2) Picking up grains of rice with knitting needles (two minutes allowed).

(3) Little bags filled with different things like coffee beans, barley, sago, salt, soda, etc. The guests must guess from the feel of the bags what is inside.

(4) Little bottles filled with different smells such as ginger, cinnamon, peppermint, coffee, verbena, ink, plain water, bovril, etc., etc.

(5) A bucketful of warm water with a silver sixpence at

the bottom. Each guest is given three pennies which they throw into the bucket, and if they succeed in covering the sixpence, it is theirs.

(6) Lighting as many candles as possible with one match. Candle rings to hold at least 40 candles can be bought or made.

Note.—It is always as well to have one or two extra prizes in reserve, as occasions arise when they are instrumental in saving ill-feeling and jealousy.

Advice to Judges : The worst decision you can possibly make is better than keeping everyone waiting.

(Signed) THE PERFECT HOSTESS.

A Cotillion Party

On arrival everyone is given a balloon, and ordinary dancing begins at once.

At 10 p.m. the Cotillion itself begins. It is important to have a rehearsal the day before with about a dozen young people, so that there is no hanging back (which can so easily ruin a party).

Two Leaders—a girl and man—must be chosen.

(1) *Grand Polonaise.* The couples march two and two in a Follow-my-leader all over the house, upstairs to the top landing and down to the kitchen, and end up by a gallop in the ballroom.

(2) *Cinderella.* Boys go out of the room, and girls throw slippers in middle of room. Boys come in and seize a slipper, and must then find the owner.

(3) Girls give boys favours and dance together.

(4) *Looking-glass.* A girl sits with her back to the room, and holds up a hand mirror. Various would-be partners look in the glass, but she passes a handkerchief across the glass, and wipes out their reflection until she is suited.

(5) Boys give girls favours and dance together.

(6) *Jockeys' Race for Partner.* The girl sits on a chair, and the men race to get there first.

(7) *Hands held over Sheet.* Girls are hidden, but their hands show over the sheet, and the boys choose their partners.

(8) *The Bogey Man.* Lights turned out. Boys put on black masks, and they dance in the dark.

GRAND GALLOP and exchange of favours.

ICES

ORDINARY DANCING

Soup, and so to Bed.

Note.—Pretty Cotillion favours can be bought inexpensively in Seven Dials.

The Domestic Staff Give a Party

DRINKS

Tea, Coffee, Lemonade, Claret Cup, Port.

SANDWICHES

Ham.
Pressed Beef and Cress.
Sausage Rolls.
Egg and Cress.
Potted Turkey and Tongue.
Sardine Rolls.

CAKES

Macaroons.
Genoa Cake.
Fruit Salad.
Iced Coffee Cake.
Ginger Biscuits.
Jellies.

Crackers.

Dancing. Games. Gramophone.

Toast of the Evening :

The Lady and Gentleman of the House.

The Courageous Game of Snapdragon

There must be many people alive to-day who have never played this old-time game, and for their benefit I propose to describe it. It was popular in the days when courage and brandy were both uncommonly cheap.

The candles were blown out, and by the blaze of the Yule Log each performer stepped forward in turn and mentally formed a Wish. On a table near the fire was a gigantic dish such as an ogre might use for his dinner-parties. The dish was filled with raisins, and over the raisins was poured brandy, which was then set alight. Into this blazing dish the performer thrust his hand in an endeavour to snatch a raisin, while the spectators encouraged his efforts, crying :

> " This Year " (for his first endeavour).
> " Some Time " (for his second effort).
> " Never " (for his third and final effort).

After that, another member of the party took his—or her—place.

A highly dangerous game, but as thrilling as a crime-movie.

For the Bone Lazy

THE EASIEST FORM OF CHILDREN'S PARTY

Suppose you live in a country town where theatres are not expensive. Engage the front row of the Dress Circle and send out invitations.

Before exclaiming : " How expensive ! " please work it out, and see if it doesn't come cheaper than a tea-party at home, where you provide tea, conjurer, flowers, extra light, help and warmth (to say nothing of the expenditure of energy).

A Cracker Party

Miss Moppytop requests
the pleasure of Master Applecheek's company
to her Cracker Party
on December 28th at 4—6.

Each child on arrival is told to look for a penny, and when found, he or she can buy three crackers from an Old Witch in one of the top rooms.

At tea, the table is decorated with every conceivable kind of cracker, containing jewels, caps, musical instruments. They must be in lavish profusion or it is not worth doing.

Dancing and games after tea, and before they go they have a " Dip " made like a gigantic cracker (blue ribbons for boys' presents and red ribbons for girls' presents).

A Five-Shilling Party

Mr. and Mrs. Merry-Gay usually give a splendid children's party at Christmas, but this year, as they could only afford to spend five shillings, the children arranged the party for themselves.

They decided to give an Arab party, because Arabs only eat dates, bananas, and spicy ginger cakes, and they only drink sherbet, which makes it much cheaper than ices and chocolate and pink sugar cakes. They dressed up as Arabs in sheets and bath-towels and bedroom slippers, and they were careful to tell their guests that their Arab costumes must be home-made. They arranged the schoolroom and dining-room to look as much like an Arab encampment as possible, with tents made of curtains and shawls, dimly lighted, and bowls of incense burning. The gramophone supplied strange Eastern music at intervals, and an obliging aunt (dressed like an Egyptian) kindly told fortunes, seated in a little alcove in semi-darkness on the stairs. Before tea they had various competitions like pinning the black beard on a sheik's head, and modelling a camel out of plasticine, etc.

After "tea" (squatting on the floor beneath several improvised tents) they had a treasure-hunt in couples. The clues took the visitors all over the house, and were distinctly Eastern in character; for instance:

(1) "By the palm tree on the mountain side" led to a small plant on the stairs.
(2) "The tribesmen gather here on a chilly night" led to the schoolroom fireplace.
(3) "The dawn finds you here" led to a bedroom.

The first prize was a small box of Turkish delight, and on it was printed the Arab proverb, "Keep your tents separate and your hearts together."

The Nursery Party Invite Us to a Concert

SUGGESTED PROGRAMME

(1) *Opening Chorus.* Old Nursery Rhyme :

Lavender's blue, diddle-diddle,
    Lavender's green.
When I am King, diddle-diddle,
    You shall be Queen.
Call up your men, diddle-diddle,
    Set them to work,
Some to the plough, diddle-diddle,
    Some to the cart,
Some to make hay, diddle-diddle,
    Some to cut corn,
While you and I, diddle-diddle,
    Keep ourselves warm.

(2) *Recitation.* (By the youngest.)

I've been good all my life,
From the hour of my birth,
I'm as good as a girl can be.
Think of all the Wicked Children
That there are upon the earth,
And THEN——Look at Me !

(Exit hurriedly.)

(3) *Dumb Act of the Knave of Hearts he Stole Some Tarts.*

(The gramophone record "Caisse Noisette" goes well with this little scene.)

(4) *Old Song.* (Little boy dressed in a smock.)

I have twelve oxen,
And they be fair and brown,
And they go a-grazing
Down by the town.
Sing Hey—Sing Ho—Sing Hoy;
Sawst you not mine oxen,
You little pretty boy?

(5) *Recitation.* (By something very young.) (Very slowly.)

When Grandma said to me one day,
"You mustn't touch the Jam,"
I did as I was bid—because
I liked the Jelly Best.

(Exit hurriedly.)

(6) *Grand Finale.* (The Golly-Wog Song in costume.)

The Nurse (grown-up) sings the solo. Each child is dressed in nightgown or pyjamas, and they each carry a candlestick. The Golly-Wog should do a little dance.

If this is considered too ambitious, they might wear nightgowns, and carry candlesticks, and recite in turn, with yawns :

" Let's off to Bed," said Sleepy Head,
" Tarry awhile," said Slow,
" Put on the Pot," says Greedy Jock,
" Let's sup before we go."
(In chorus) " Good-night, Everybody."

(EXIT.)

Christmas Theatricals

Christmas Theatricals

Few things are more amusing than amateur theatricals, but nothing leads to more ill-feeling.

It is essential to choose a Stage Manager as much like Mussolini or Napoleon as possible, and his word must be LAW. Simple tact in dealing with amateurs is about as much use as in dealing with tigers.

On Choosing a Play. Choose a short clever play *that acts itself*, and avoid elaborate scenic effects.

A Variety Entertainment is far easier to arrange, as if one performer falls out, the evening is not seriously upset. It could include two short plays and various numbers from Musical Comedies. This will give scope for a chorus of pretty girls and young men.

I would suggest the following programme :

1. *Opening Chorus.* Either original, or copied from the Follies or Co-Optimists.
2. *Song.*
3. *Apache Dance* (Allows great scope for talent).
4. *Playlet.*

INTERVAL AND ICES.

5. *Song.*
6. *Old English Songs* acted in costume, such as " My Man John " or " Oh, no, John ; no, John ; no, John."
7. *Playlet.*
8. *A Burlesque of Old-fashioned Dances*, such as the Washington Post, the Pas de Quatre, the old Hop Waltz, down to the modern Tango. As each dance ends, the new couple should come on saying something disparaging about the last couple. The modern couple must be tremendously off-hand to each other.
9. *Grand Finale.* If it can be done, nothing is as good as an Epilogue with " local " jokes, but if that is not practicable, then a cheerful number should be chosen from some well-known and recent " hit " in which the audience can join.

WHAT NOT TO HAVE

1. Opening : A piano solo in five movements.

(Long wait.)

2. (*a*) Sentimental Song.
   (*b*) Warlike Song.
   (*c*) Simple little Ditty.

(Long wait.)

3. Amateur Conjurer, whose tricks take hours, and then fail.

(Long wait.)

4. Ambitious Play written by the hostess, with no point.

(Long wait.)

5. Recitations, which make the audience wish to sink through the floor with embarrassment.

(Long wait.)

6. Child's impersonation of Dickens' Character.

(Long wait.)

7. Glee Singers, all out of tune.

(Long wait.)

8. More card tricks that don't come off.

(Long wait.)

9. Mandoline or banjolele solo by someone who has had twelve easy lessons.

(Long wait.)

10. Grand Finale. Soldiers' Chorus from "Faust" in costume, finishing up with a lengthy speech by Host to audience already fainting with boredom.

The Grand Transformation Scene

A transformation scene makes such a magnificent end to an evening's charades that I must include it.

The expense is nil, but a certain amount of ingenuity is required.

In regard to " props," it is best to make a tour of the house earlier in the day, and collect anything gorgeous or shiny. Tea-cosys make splendid Balkan headdresses and brass fire-irons look like sceptres and tridents. Brass flower-pots on the head give a regal effect, and a fur rug will be a splendid train for Canada's queen or the Lion of Old England.

It is necessary to obtain a gramophone record of " Tunes of all Nations."

A large Chesterfield sofa must be placed in the centre of the stage and the Transformation Scene is now ready.

The Good Fairy (man or woman) stands at the side, and announces in a triumphant voice : " Gallant Little Wales," or " Bonny Scotland," or " The Star-Spangled Banner," according to the tune that the gramophone is blaring out. At his words, two people (you won't be able to afford more) step out bravely from behind the scene and mount the back of the Chesterfield. They are followed by two other " Countries," who sit on the arms in heroic attitudes : two others seat themselves on the cushions. This must all be done with a great flourish, and the stage is in constant movement, as the first couple have to nip out smartly in order to reappear as " Brave little Belgium " or " Gay Paree " a few seconds later.

N.B.—The audience are likely to recognise the performers after their third or fourth appearance and are apt to call each other's attention to the fact.

For the final curtain, the Fairy Queen must place herself (or himself) in the centre of the group, and they all salute. At this moment a small messenger boy brings in a telegram, and the Good Fairy reads out some appropriate message to the audience.

God Save the King.

Christmas Charity

Old Song

Christmas is coming, and the geese are getting fat,
Please to put a penny in the old man's hat.
If you haven't got a penny, a halfpenny will do.
If you haven't got a halfpenny—
God Bless you !

The English Gentleman and Pol Roger Champagne -
The Perfect Christmas combination

Lest We Forget

The form which our Christmas Charity is to take is a question for us each to decide. Since our hearts are small, it is inevitable that we sympathise—or "tune into"—certain kinds of Hard Luck cases more readily than to others.

Here is a short handy list ready for use (and please don't put it off until you forget all about it):

Do you "tune into" Old Jockeys?

The Bentinck Benevolent Fund,
15, Cavendish Square, W.1.

Do you "tune into" Old Seamen?

Royal Alfred Aged Merchant Seamen Institution,
58, Fenchurch Street, E.C.3.

Do you "tune into" Old Actors?

Actors' Benevolent Fund,
8, Adam Street,
Adelphi, W.C. 2.

Do you "tune into" Old Governesses?

Governess' Benevolent Institution,
Dacre House,
5, Arundel Street,
Strand, W.C.2.

Do you "tune into" Old Cab-drivers?

Cab-drivers' Benevolent Association,
18, Soho Square, W.

Are you fond of reading?

Old Librarians' Fund, Institute of Journalists,
Tudor Street, E.C.4.

Do you like being a " friend in need " ?

The Friends of the Poor,
40, Ebury Street, S.W.

There are hundreds of other excellent charities, more widely known, but I have chosen these to save you the trouble of looking up addresses.

Presents

Who'll Buy—Who'll Buy?

The satisfaction of things well done and the prospect of a Perfect Christmas

Make a Note

(1) Send out the Christmas Pudding in good time to sons and nephews in regiments and ships abroad (the Post Office thoughtfully supplies a list of dates).

(2) If a child has 'flu or measles, and cannot come to your party, make up an exciting parcel of the crackers, Christmas presents and oddments she would have had and send it to her, with a little note.

(3) Do you know any old soul in an Almshouse who would be cheered all through the year by a subscription to a weekly newspaper? Say a sporting paper to an old bed-ridden jockey, or a "fashion and society" weekly to a retired lady's maid, or some Australian or Canadian paper to an old Colonist.

(4) Order an inexpensive posy of flowers to be sent every Saturday to a very old lady. Even the simplest flowers are welcome, and it is something for her to look forward to.

(5) Arrange for boxing, tennis or cricket coaching for your favourite godson, and consult him on the choice.

(6) Give your grown-up niece a course of first-rate dressmaking lessons.

(7) Send letters and parcels in *Good Time* to distant friends—it makes all the difference.

(8) Invite at least one stranger-in-the-land to a friendly meal, and don't assume that someone else is sure to look after them.

(9) If you are sending any useful gifts to the local workhouse, find out if there is any Come-down-in-the-world, and send him six handkerchiefs, nice soap and sponge, good tooth-powder and brush, razor and shaving soap, and a pack of cards—the sort of things you would like yourself under the circumstances.

(10) Pay all small tradesmen's debts.

(11) Make up any stray quarrels you have on hand.

(12) Buy yourself a nice present as a reward.

The Perfect Present: (A fact.)

A Dustman: I GIVES MY MISSUS A FIVE-PUN' NOTE AN NO QUESTIONS ASKED.

Presents for the Head of the House

A new or old book on his favourite subject—Bridge, golf, travel, fishing, shooting, dogs, wild animals, warfare, gardening or flying.

Golf balls. Tennis racquet and balls.

Pot of foie gras. Stilton Cheese. Caviar.

Two tickets for any play he likes to choose.

Silk handkerchiefs, pyjamas, bright bath-towels, chamois leather gloves.

Ki-uma bath tablets or a large sponge.

An order on the hat shop in St. James's Street for a new hat.

Cigarettes, or six super-superb Cigars.*

Bottle of Sherry.*

½ ton of Peat to make him happy, and revive memories.

Note.—DON'T GIVE HIM A TIE. BRACES ARE MUCH MORE USEFUL.

Presents for Madame

Linen table mats.

Silk stockings.

Large glass flower bowls.

A brass toasting fork.

A set of Pyrex glass.

A blue Morocco suitcase, costing about a pound.

An early morning tea-set for her own use.

A new cookery book.

A set of address books marked Friends—Tradesmen—Hotels, etc.

A set of scissors.

Fantasie Bath Salts.

* Be careful of the brand.

Umbrella: or *en-tous-cas*.

A year's subscription to "Vogue" or "The Times' Literary Supplement"—or both.

A cover for her Telephone Book.

A box of large assorted envelopes, together with a sealing set.

Flowers—in small or large quantities.

The One-Present Man

Some of the most intelligent of men are capable of thinking of *one* present only, and this they send to each of their friends. I append a short list for the One-present man to choose from:

A 5*s*. Book of Stamps. (This is wildly popular among the recipients.)

A Ham.

A Tongue.

A Jar of Ginger.

7 lbs. of Jackson's Earl Grey Tea.

Violets (fresh).

Crystallised Fruits.

A large Pineapple.

Guava Jelly.

Stilton Cheese.

Maple Syrup or Narbonne Honey.

365 Pencils for the year.

Presents for the Golf Maniac

(1) 1 dozen Balls.

(2) 1 pair Chamois Gloves.

(3) 1 pair Hand-knitted Golf Stockings.

(4) 1 Belt for purse and tees.

(5) Pair of Mittens.

(6) A good Book on Golf.

(7) A year's subscription to the best Golf Paper.
(8) An Engagement Book with Golf Fixtures.
(9) A Pull-over.
(10) A Golf Umbrella.

Presents We Don't Want

(1) Chocolates with hard centres.
(2) Bright Cushions (that match nothing in the house).
(3) Complicated apparatus for licking stamps.
(4) Fountain Pens that leak.
(5) Penwipers—Biscuit Barrels—useless ornaments in shapes of pigs, cats, etc.
(6) Book Ends that are too light.
(7) Dressing Bags that are too heavy.

Presents for Schoolboys

A pair of Handcuffs (most popular).
A Silver Watch.
A Knife.
A set of Meccano.
A Kodak (with year's upkeep).
Fountain Pen.
Book on their special subject.
Pistol with caps.
Small Rifle.
Box of Conjuring Tricks.
Box of Chemistry outfit.
Red Indian Tent.
Red Indian Suit.
Tram Conductor Outfit.
Jigsaw Puzzles.
Wire Puzzles.
Roller Skates.
Real Ice Skates.
Chocolate Drops covered with hundreds and thousands.

Presents for Schoolgirls

Stuffed Comic Animal.
Extra long-legged Doll.
Own Tea-set.
Fitted Pencil Case.
Note-paper with initial.
Book (if carefully chosen).
Watch or Clock.
Purse with money in it (*not* empty).
Bright Scarf.
Hockey Stick.
Autograph Album.
A Diary and Confession Book.
A ticket for herself and a friend (to be chosen by herself) for a play.
Travelling Photo Frame.
Umbrella.
Sealing-wax Set.
Jewel Case with secret drawer.
Gramophone Record.
Chocolate Drops covered with hundreds and thousands.

Presents for the Domestic Staff

Despatch Case in blue morocco, costing about 8*s*. 6*d*.
Gloves lined with fur.
A small Tea-set of their own.
A comfortable Armchair or Cushion.
An Eiderdown in pretty colours.
An Umbrella, Goloshes, Mackintosh.

Cheaper Presents.

Pretty Blotter and Inkpot.
(Not handkerchiefs, as they are too hackneyed.)
Money in a small purse.
Pot of growing flowers.
1 doz. pretty Pencils and Notebook for shopping.
Cream for their hands, and two pairs of Chamois Gloves.
Manicure Set.
Pretty Sponge Bag with coloured sponge and face towel.
Pretty Bedroom Shoes.

The Schoolroom Faces the Economic Situation and Makes Presents

FOR THE CLEVER-FINGERED

Barbola Buttonholes. The flowers are modelled from Barbola (8*d.* a tin) and stuck on green wire for stems. When the flowers are hard, they are painted with Poster Colours (6*d.* a tube) and varnished with Barbola varnish (8*d.* a bottle).

Whitewood Boxes, Book-ends, etc. These can be painted with either " Newinlac " (6*d.* a bottle) or sealing-wax paint (made from dissolving Dennison's wax in methylated spirit). Before being painted they should have a coat of " Filler " (1*s.* a bottle), and then be well sandpapered with fine sandpaper to get a perfectly smooth surface. Last of all, they can be decorated with Poster Colours, Barbola, or sealing-wax.

" *Docora* " *Ware Matchboxes, Telephone Blocks, etc.* These can be decorated with sealing-wax, sealing-wax paint, or ordinary water-colours.

Wallets, Tobacco Pouches, Purses, etc. can be made quite easily from suede leather, if you have a puncher (price about 2*s*. 6*d*. or 3*s*. 6*d*.), but the leather is rather expensive.

Pictures framed with Passe-partout (6*d*. a roll), and with or without calendars attached, make very nice inexpensive presents.

Needlework. Handkerchief and glove sachets, linen tray-cloths, pincushions, *pochettes* with Zip fasteners, covered coat-hangers, tie-cases, gardening aprons. Recipe books, covers for telephone books, etc., etc.

FOR THE CLUMSY-FINGERED

Blotters. Just blotting-paper folded and tied with ribbon, and a picture stuck on the outside.

Calendars. A picture stuck on cardboard, with a calendar attached.

"*Decora*" *Ware Matchboxes* with sealing-wax flowers on them.

Wool Flowers made from circles of cardboard covered with wool and then cut away. Big balls for very young children can be made in the same way.

Lavender Bags made from circles of mauve muslin, tied with mauve ribbon.

Needle-cases. Pen-wipers from felt. Cross-stitch on canvas for kettle-holders, etc.

Not to be Read by Grown-ups

Pennies for Presents

Any shop selling wallpapers will let you have an " out of stock " roll for threepence (I shouldn't be surprised if you were given it for nothing). Paste the wallpaper carefully on to any old milliner's hat-box or dress-box, and don't forget to paste a small stick-on label on the side, so that Mummie, on going to her boxroom, can read on her pretty boxes, " Last Summer's green hat " or " Pink evening frock."

A welcome present for Daddy, costing threepence :—No father in the country has enough ash-trays, so you can make one for his special writing-table. Buy a small glass jam dish for twopence, and a pennyworth of varnish. Paste inside the dish a layer of brightly coloured tinfoil (such as you get wrapped round chocolates) and varnish it over. This is very effective as it is, but if you have any gold paint in your possession you can get a very gorgeous effect by painting the outside of the glass gold, and varnishing it in the same way.

A present for Aunt Lavinia, costing threepence :—Buy a packet of bright blue luggage labels, a packet of stick-on labels and a sheet of bright blue blotting-paper. Make a cover by sewing any scrap of cretonne or linen crash over stiff cardboard and lightly tack the blotting-paper and labels inside.

A present for little Moppytop, costing only time and trouble :—Do you prefer black or brown Topsy dolls ? If you like black best, use a black stocking ; if you prefer brown, then you must use an old brown stocking. Stuff it carefully and make the legs and arms separately. For the head tie a ribbon tightly round the neck, and make the eyes of small linen buttons with a nice expression inked on the centre ; black mending wool for the hair (either bobbed or in long plaits), red turkey cotton for the rosebud mouth and nostrils. If possible make a frock of the same material as worn by Miss Moppytop herself.

The House at Christmas Time

To the Maids

Wash your hands, or else the fire
Will not teind to your desire.
Unwasht hands, ye maidens, know,
Dead the fire, though ye blow.

HERRICK.

The Christmas Drawer

Every house should contain at least one drawer devoted to Christmas requirements.

Balls of coloured string.
Fancy Christmas paper for wrapping up parcels.
Gold braid for tying up special gifts.
Luggage labels with holly pattern.
Blotting-paper and a good supply of pens, ink and paper.
Tissue-paper.
Various sized cardboard boxes (may be kept one inside the other).
Sealing-wax.
Corrugated paper.
Ball of strong string.
Sheets of brown paper (strong).
Large pair of scissors tied with red ribbon (to prevent your family from annexing them).
India-rubber (for rubbing out prices).*
Little roll of cotton wool for precious parcels.
Your own visiting cards.

* *Note.*—It's quite useless to rub out 6½*d.* and write 7*s.* 6*d.* Everyone knows the make and values far too well these days !

Decorating the House

The chief points, if you wish to be successful in your decorations, is to confine your activities to certain rooms and to do them lavishly.

I would suggest :

The Hall.
The Dining-room.
The Schoolroom.
The Nursery.
The Servants' Hall.

It is a good idea to have a " Set Piece " in each room where the eye can focus. I would suggest :

A Christmas Tree in the Hall made to look as snowy as possible by non-inflammable cotton wool and decorated with coloured balls and tinsel. Mistletoe over the door, and holly on all the pictures. The table where letters and small parcels are usually placed might be covered with a scarlet cloth for this week only. Red electric or lamp-shades carry out the scheme.

The Dining-room. The " set piece " here must inevitably be the dining-table. Red candles in silver candlesticks and red poinsettias for a formal dinner—small Christmas figures of Santa Claus, reindeer, sledges and snowy cottages for other occasions; a hunting scene or a decorated " candle-ring " all make a gay scene. Holly on all the pictures.

The Schoolroom. Be very lavish with the decorations here. A bunch of different coloured balloons suspended from the ceiling give a festive air even if they have a habit of " popping " occasionally (they can be replaced). Mistletoe over the door—holly on the walls. A jar of honesty in the window, and a pot of growing red tulips near it for contrast.

The Nursery. The Nursery must have its own miniature Christmas tree, about 2 feet high, and the children should be allowed to decorate it and re-decorate it as often as they like. They may like to give their pet animals and favourite dolls " a Christmas party," in which case they will be happy for days making suitable presents.

In the corner of the Nursery there should be a little Manger with the Holy Figures, and this will be treated with great reverence.

Holly and mistletoe arranged with care on the pictures.

The Servants' Hall. May I suggest that the Domestic Staff be given the money, and allowed to buy their own decorations ? An afternoon should be set aside for the purpose.

Before Christmas

Have you enough *Soda-Water ?*
Have you ordered in Coal and Coke ?
Have you enough Cakes, Biscuits, provisions in tins and Whisky ?
Extra Blankets and Eiderdowns for unexpected guests ?

HAVE YOU ENOUGH CIGARETTES ?

Enough scissors, pencils and stacks of note-paper ?
Have you enough SODA-WATER ?
Enough Toilet Soap ?
Sheets and Towels ?
Have you enough Stamps, Stamps, Stamps ?
Have you enough Cigarettes ?

ONE MOMENT PLEASE—THE SODA-WATER !

Clearing Up After Christmas

Christmas festivities have a way of permeating every corner of the house, and nothing is more depressing than dead evergreens and burst balloons.

(1) Press all the family into the general clear up, and do room by room.

(2) Start by taking down evergreens and all decorations.

(3) Remove Christmas cards from chimney-piece, and put in drawer for a wet day.

(4) All brown paper and string to be collected and stored in drawer.

(5) Make up a parcel of decorations and odds and ends for the Hospital Party.

(6) Send off rubbish to the Jumble Sale.

(7) Make up a parcel for the cleaners, as Christmas time is unusually heavy on clothes.

(8) If you are a woman, set aside the following day for Beauty Treatment, as prolonged festivities are very ageing.

(9) Engage a competent charwoman to help the exhausted staff clean and sweep.

Note.—Charwomen who can tell fortunes out of tea-leaves are much in demand, but the less gifted kind are quicker over their work.

What to do with Rubbish

Never, never, never give away as presents rubbish or monstrosities you have bought at bazaars.

"That will do for old Aunt Susan," you say as you look loathingly at a plush handkerchief sachet; or, "The very thing for Uncle Albert," as you seize a dust-catching newspaper stand.

The only thing to do with rubbish is:

(A) Put it in your Ideal Boiler.
(B) Send it to a Jumble Sale.
(C) Give it to the Rag and Bone Man on his next visit.

Note.—If anyone sends you rubbish as a Christmas present, put it in the fire, and send a telegram of thanks. If that doesn't make them feel ashamed, I don't know what will:

Ex.—"Thousand thanks for shell pincushion stuck on pill-box."

or,

Reply Paid: "Gilded Pinecones safely received; what are they for?"

Note.—Present-giving is *not* a question of money but of common-sense.

In the Best Regulated Families, Accidents will Occur

THE MEDICINE CHEST

A thermometer.
A medicine glass.
Iodine.
Boracic Powder.
Boracic Ointment.
Zinc Ointment.
Carron Oil, for burns.
A camel's hair paint-brush for removing things from the eye.
Bandages and Lint.
Sticking Plaster.
Newskin.
Iodex, for bruises.
Pond's Extract (Cream).
Vinolia.
Pair of scissors, needle and thread, safety-pins.
Tweezers.
Friar's Balsam.
Singleton's Golden Ointment at first suggestion of styes.
Castor Oil.
Eno's Fruit Salt.
Calomel.
Vapex.
Ammoniated Quinine.
Elliman's Embrocation.
Aspirin.
Bismuth.
Vaseline.
Sal Volatile.
Brandy.

Paste in the lid of the chest " What to do in Emergencies," and also the name, address and telephone number of the nearest doctor and chemist.

The Bursting Pipe

Why do pipes so often burst on Boxing Day, when no plumbers are available ?

This is one of the mysteries of life, and my own belief is that pipes do not like festivities, and always try to wreck them.

It would save a lot of expense if the hostess would have a competent plumber in to advise her of the weak spots before the thaw occurs, so that she may have the danger spots wrapped up in straw, and a small oil stove burning through the night. I will not promise that the stove will not be in league with the pipes, and avenge them by smoking all night, and covering the bathroom with a film of greasy black.

This is a very black page.

The Money Question

A great deal must be said for being methodical over money at Christmas. It is easy for expenses to run up in a surprising way, and one can obtain very little result. On the other hand, by careful planning it is amazing what can be done.

Do let me entreat every head of family to put aside the amount he can afford, and apportion it out after a family consultation. It might be arranged as follows :—

	£ s. d.
Presents	
Stamps	
Cards and Calendars . . .	
Our Party	
Extra Food	
Extra Wine	
Extra Domestic Help . . .	
Extra Transport (a large item) . .	
Charity	
Pantomime	
Extra Games	
Extra Firing and Lighting . .	
Flowers and Decorations . . .	
Sundries	
Total	£

How to Waste Money

(1) Order in a lot of fruit that goes bad.

(2) Order in flowers you have no time to arrange.

(3) Buy handsome presents and have them put down.

(4) Give a big Dance when you can only afford a Games Evening.

(5) Economise on heating, and give everyone 'flu (see Doctors', Nurses' bills).

(6) Economise on lighting (and let people trip over stairs and break their ankles, etc.).

(7) Give rubbishy presents and make lifelong enemies.

(8) Overdo yourself and have to go into a Nursing Home.

Roses in December

For Hostesses who must have things out of season.

During the last days of September gather twelve rosebuds, which must have long stalks and be tightly shut. Place them in warm water for an hour. Then wrap them in cotton wool and put them in a long tin box, sticking adhesive plaster round the edges of the lid.

Bury the box eighteen inches below ground.

On Christmas morning dig up the box and plunge the roses into water.

Note.—They will only last six hours, so you must time the hour of their disinterment with care if you wish to say casually at dinner, " Yes, these came out of our garden. I got them this afternoon," etc., etc.

Here We Come a Whistling

Here we come a whistling through the fields so green;
Here we come a singing, so fair to be seen.
God send you happy, God send you happy,
Pray God send you a happy New Year !

The roads are very dirty, my boots are very thin,
I have a little pocket to put a penny in,
God send you happy, God send you happy,
Pray God send you a happy New Year !

Bring out your little table and spread it with a cloth,
Bring out some of your old ale, likewise your Christmas loaf.
God send you happy, God send you happy,
Pray God send you a happy New Year !

God bless the master of this house, likewise the mistress too ;
And all the little children that round the table strew.
God send you happy, God send you happy,
Pray God send you a happy New Year !

The cock sat up in the yew tree,
The hen came chuckling by ;
I wish you a merry Christmas,
And a good fat pig in the sty.

From "A Christmas Garland, Carols and Poems."—BULLEN.

Games

For a Perfect Christmas go by Lotus

LOTUS CARS LIMITED · NORWICH · NORFOLK · ENGLAND NR14 8EZ

Indoor Games

(Which every House, large or small, should possess at Christmas time.)

Ping-Pong.
Bagatelle.
The Racing Game (or its variations).
Ludo.
Chess.
Draughts.
Tiddlywinks.
Halma.
Pipes for blowing bubbles.
Book of Crossword Puzzles.

Note.—Wet afternoons lose their terror if you can hastily arrange a " games tournament " to take place in different rooms in the house.

Charades

Charades are most popular, and may either be rehearsed beforehand or impromptu.

Here is a suggestion. The word chosen is "Tutankhamen."

1st Scene. *Toot.* Actors in car tooting loudly.

2nd Scene. *Tank.* Actors in war-time *tank* going over the ground.

3rd Scene. *Ah.* Actors dressed as sightseers at a Gallery, exclaiming "Ah, AH, AH" in front of some picture.

4th Scene. *Men.* Girls waiting disconsolate for partners at a dance, when suddenly two men appear and there is nearly a free fight.

Final Word. *Tutankhamen.* Someone wrapped in a sheet on the table, and the others dressed as Egyptians watching round the mummy.

Aeroplane.

Air. Nervous lady fainting at a concert, and calling for air.

O. Someone trying to telephone a telegram for a box of oysters or oranges.

Plane (plain). A beauty competition at a local fair.

Final Word. *Aeroplane.* A meeting of the War Cabinet to discuss the aeroplane form of attack.

Piccadilly.

Pick. Scene—Convicts at work at Dartmoor.

A. Deaf old man who can only say "Eh?" when various people try to tell him he has won the Calcutta Sweepstake.

Dilly. Party of village glee singers rendering "Fair Daffodils, we weep to see you," and alternately, "Dilly, Dilly, Dilly, come and be killed, for you must be stuffed and my customers filled."

Final Word. Piccadilly. Scene on Underground Railway with lost travellers trying to find their way out to Regent Street and Shaftesbury Avenue, with a comic policeman in evidence.

OTHER USEFUL WORDS

Con-tempt-ible.
Night-in-gale.
Prim-rose.
Cow-ard-ice.
Con-ceit.
Del-i-cate.
Coal-box.
Friend-ship.

Snap-dragon.
Par-lia-ment.
Wire-less.
In-quire.
Pan-try.
So-fa.
Pig-tail.
Art-i-choke.

Wel-come.

Card Games for the Nursery and Schoolroom

Beggar my Neighbour.
Fours.
Aces.
Courted, Cried and Married.
My Bird Sings.
Thank You.
Old Maid.
Snap, with variations of Singing Snap.
Rummy.
Schoolroom Poker.
Donkey.
Pelman Patience.
Racing Demon.
Throwing cards into a hat.
Angry Monkey.
Cork Grab.

Games for the Rather Young

Do not forget that the Younger Folk all frankly hate " writing games," and the early part of each evening should be devoted to their amusement. (Once they have safely said good-night, we can make a rush for pencil and paper.)

THE PRINCE OF WALES HAS LOST HIS HAT

Chairs are named Red Hat, Green Hat, etc.

The Prince sits in middle and starts :

" The Prince of Wales has lost his Hat, and some say this and some say that, but I say Red Hat."

Red Hat : " I, sir ? "

Prince : " Yes, you, sir ! "

Red Hat : " Not I, sir."

Prince : " Who then, sir ? "

Red Hat : " Blue Hat, sir."

Blue Hat : " I, sir ? "

Red Hat : " Yes, you, sir," etc., etc.

Player making a mistake moves down to the bottom and all move up. The Prince starts game again. A player can say " Prince, sir," etc., when the Prince must answer. Answer must be correct and must be made before questioner counts *ten.* If Prince is caught he goes to the bottom, and questioner becomes Prince.

You had better simplify the answers if the players are very young.

HEARTH BRUSH

A beautiful game. You take a perfectly common black hearth brush (the taller the better) and balance it on its bristles. You all take hands and dance round it and try to make each other touch it sufficiently hard to upset it. If very little ones are playing, it is sometimes possible to lift them bodily over the brush when they are in danger. As each one knocks down the brush they retire, until the victor is left triumphant.

RIVAL BANDS

The party divides into bands. Then the respective bandmasters each send one of their bandsmen out of the room. The rival bands hide a thimble in the usual manner, and then call in the two outside together to search for it.

Each band chooses a different tune which they hum to encourage their man (*loud* when he is far from the thimble, *soft* when he is near). When the thimble is found, both searchers go to the winning band, and two others are sent out.

N.B.—This is not a game for musical people.

POOR PUSSY

All sit round in a circle, Poor Pussy in the centre. Pussy cries " Mieou, Mieou," to one of the others, who strokes Pussy, saying sympathetically, " Poor Pussy, Poor Pussy," but keeping a grave face.

Pussy's idea is to make him smile, and this he does by mieouing plaintively or contentedly or occasionally giving vent to a *scat*. If the other smiles, he becomes Poor Pussy in turn.

AN OLD FAVOURITE

A. My great-great-grandmother died and left me a pair of scissors (with two fingers makes motion of cutting).

B. My great-great-grandmother died and left me a pair of scissors and a sewing machine (makes motion of cutting, plus treadle with feet).

C. My great-great-grandmother died and left me a pair of scissors, a sewing machine and a fan (action with scissors, sewing machine and fan).

D. My great-great-grandmother died and left me a pair of scissors, a sewing machine, a fan, and a rocking chair, etc.

E. My great-great-grandmother died and left me a pair of scissors, a sewing machine, a fan, a rocking chair and a nodding Chinese mandarin, etc.

A SHORT LIST OF WELL-KNOWN GAMES

Oranges and Lemons.
Twos and Threes.
Dumb Crambo.
Tod Tiddler's Ground.
Pop goes the Weasel.
Nuts and May.
General Post.
Puss in the Corner.
When I was a Lady.
Spin the Platter.
Musical Bumps.
Cobbler, Cobbler, mend my Shoe.
I wrote a Letter to my Love.

FINALLY

Sir Roger de Coverley.

The Game of Miss Nomer

You take it in turns to find a misnomer, and pay a forfeit when you cannot think of one.

I know a Miss Young who is very old.
I know a Miss Sharp who is very blunt.
I know a Miss Short who is very tall.
I know a Miss Best who is very bad.
I know a Miss Courage who is very timid.

(You must, of course, use only well-known surnames.)

The Game of Miss Representation

You each go out of the room in turn, and dress up as

(A) A mutual friend,
(B) A living celebrity, or
(C) Each other.

The others guess who you represent, and I will not guarantee it does not lead to ill-feeling. But it is a most amusing game.

The Joyous and Noisy Game of School

The players sit in a long line (youngest top) with the schoolmistress facing them. The game should be played at top speed. Anyone who fails to answer a question moves down a place, and the teacher can also send anyone to the bottom for shouting or not attending. At the end of three minutes the top pupil takes the place of the teacher. To begin with, a letter of the alphabet is chosen, and all answers must begin with that letter. For example, the letter " B."

Teacher : There was once a ship called . . . ?
1st Pupil : The Bonnie Bessy.
Teacher : And where was it built ?
2nd Pupil : At Bath.
Teacher : No, they don't build ships at Bath. Next, please.
3rd Pupil : At Bristol (goes up one).
Teacher : What was the Captain's name ?
4th Pupil : Captain Barnstaple.
Teacher : Yes, but what was his wife's pet name for him ?
5th Pupil : Bunker !
Teacher : No, that's not a pet name.

Sixth and Seventh both miss, but Eighth says " Biffkins," and goes up three places.

Teacher : What was the Captain's favourite expression ?
9th Pupil : Bless my buttons.
Teacher : And what was the weather like ?
Pupil : Beautiful.
Teacher : Yes, but then it changed and became . . . ?
Pupil : Beastly (is sent down one place for talking slang).
Teacher : What was the sailors' favourite amusement ?
Pupil : Playing billiards.
Teacher : No, they couldn't play billiards at sea. Next, please.
Pupil (brilliantly) : " Bull-board." (He is sent to the top for this bright effort, to the intense indignation of the top pupil, who is thereupon sent to the bottom for talking.)
Teacher : What cargo did they carry ?
Pupil : Bead necklaces for savages.
Teacher : Yes, and what else ?
Pupil : Beetles !
Teacher : Certainly not ! Move down one for answering foolishly. Etc., etc., etc.

Forfeits

" First catch your forfeits," as the old recipe began, so we will begin with the good old game of Family Coach.

FAMILY COACH

Someone is the story-teller, and the rest balance themselves on and round the Chesterfield. Each chooses some part of the coach, or members of the family entering the coach.

Example : Box seat. Henry.
Wheels. Thomas.
Picnic basket. Mary.
Baby. Philip.
Coachman. Aunt Eliza.
Reins. Pamela.
Whip. Sholto.
Axle pole. James.
Etc., etc.

When the story-teller mentions anyone's name-part, they must get up quickly, and turn round and sit down again. When he says " Family Coach," everybody must *get up and turn round.*

Ex. " On a dark and stormy night, the *father* sent word to the *coachman* that the *family coach* was to be ready at once. But the *coachman* found that one *wheel* was off," etc., etc.

Anyone failing to get up pays a forfeit.

And here we come to the polite game of

FORFEITS

1. One person buries his head in the lap of " The Mother," who holds up a forfeit, saying : " Here is a thing and a very pretty thing. What shall the owner of this pretty thing do ? "

Ans. " Bow to the wittiest, kneel to the prettiest, kiss the one he likes best."

2. *Polish Beggars:* (Two forfeits are cried at once.) The two beggars must go to the others in turn. The elder beggar says: "Please could you spare a little something for myself and my wife?" If the answer is a box on the ears, he passes it on to his wife; if it is a kiss, he also passes it on, and so on until he has completed the circle.

3. *Cutting the Bacon:* The owner of the forfeit is sent into the corner. He pretends to cut bacon by the simple process of crossing his fingers, at the same time crying plaintively:

> "I stand in the corner and cut bacon.
> Whoever loves me will take me away."

He stays in the corner, becoming more and more pathetic, until someone takes pity and fetches him away.

4. *Truth:* The forfeit owner goes out of the room, and the others think out three questions which must be answered *truthfully*.

5. *A Penance:* *Dance* in one corner; *Sing* in another; *Recite* in a third, and *Make a polite bow* in the fourth.

6. *Gossip:* The forfeit owner goes out of the room, and on his return he is told:

> *Somebody said you were very conceited, or charming, or good at cracking nuts, or opening windows, or blacking boots.*

He bows to the one he thinks has said this, and if he is wrong, the others hiss. If he guesses right, the others clap.

Rummy

Everyone appears to play Rummy differently. Here is the right way.

For three, four or more players. If there are more than four it is advisable to have two packs of cards.

Cut for deal as usual.

The cards are dealt three—two—three, so that each player has a hand of eight cards.

The next card is turned face upwards and placed by the side of the undealt cards.

A stake from each player is put into the pool. It may be just as small or as big as the players like.

The Game

The object of each player is to get rid of cards, and cards are got rid of by being in threes or in sequences. If you have three eights you have a " three " and can discard. A sequence may be as long as your hand but it must not be less than three cards: 5, 6, 7 for instance; or 9, 10, knave, queen. Sequences like " threes " don't count—they are discarded.

The twos can be considered anything, so that there are in effect four jokers in the pack.

The Play

The hands are dealt. You are the " age "—next the dealer. You examine your eight cards to see if you have a sequence or three of a kind. *Always remember the two.* You may have a good hand—two " threes " and two small cards, a 4 and a 3. If the others start changing they may get rid of their cards before you. Actually you have only 4 and 3 to count; somebody must have more than seven, and so you expose your hand at once without exchanging a card. The pips are counted and everybody's score is taken. In that respect it is like dominoes.

The score is usually fixed at 100, though if there are six players or more it may be better to increase it to 125 or 150.

The cards are dealt again. This time your hand is not so good. You can exchange one of your cards for either the one exposed or for the one unexposed on the top of the pack. Obviously you won't take the exposed one if it wouldn't be any good to you. You take the one on the top of the pack, putting one from your hand in its place. You do not expose the card you have taken nor the one you have put in its place. If you exchange with the exposed one your discard is also exposed.

The sequences and threes are put face upwards on the table.

This exchanging of cards goes round the table till somebody declares, which means that a player considers his hand likely to be the lowest and wishes the others to stop bettering theirs. After a declaration by a player that he will show his cards the round of exchanging must be completed.

If the pack threatens to get exhausted the discarded sequences and threes are shuffled and used with the remainder of the pack.

Scoring

When a player scores the full points (100, 125 or 150) he drops out. He may come to life again; that is, he may continue by paying into the pool another stake (equal to the original) and assuming a score equal to that of the highest player.

Note.—It is easier to make sequences than threes. It is well to keep an eye on the discards.

In counting, all court cards equal tens.

When someone declares and is beaten he pays half a stake in the pool. The pips are counted as usual. Suppose you have a score of nine (and anything below ten, especially on a first hand, is good), you may gamble that the others will be over that, and as you want to catch them with as big a score as possible you declare and so prevent the drawing of cards. Remember that if someone has already exchanged a card, though you may declare, that round of exchanging is completed and then the cards are shown.

Riddles and Worse

"Wouldn't it have been a good idea to have first contacted Burke's Peerage about a coat of arms for Christmas?"

Riddles and Worse

I hear the N eu-riches' Garage cost more to build than Windsor Castle!

Really!

Yes, you see Windsor Castle was built for a Sovereign.

What is the difference between a tiger and a bison?

A tiger is a wild animal, and a bison is the thing you wash your hands in.

(Apologies to people with refained accents.)

What goes up white and comes down yellow?

An egg.

(*Note.*—Please do not experiment on the best carpet.)

Formed long ago and yet made to-day,
Employed while others sleep.
What few would like to give away
Nor any wish to keep.

A comfortable bed.

What is that which gives a cold, cures a cold and pays the doctor?

A draft.

A Shocking Page

Did you hear the story of the empty Christmas stocking ?
No ?
Oh, there was nothing in it !

Did you hear the story of the two eggs ?
No.
Ah ! Two bad !

How to Prove the Moon is made of Green Cheese.

You'll agree that either it is or it isn't made of green cheese ?
Certainly.
Well, it isn't made of green cheese, is it ?
No.
Therefore it is !

How's ginger ?
Ginger who ?
Ginger yourself when you fell off your bicycle ? (Did you injure yourself, etc.)

Have you seen Teresa Green ?
No, I have not seen the trees are green.

What did the donkey say when given his favourite food ?
Thistle do.

How do you pronounce " Sabots " in English ?
I should pronounce it wooden shoe, wouldn't you ?

Catches that Break up Families

(*Answers on page* 151)

(1) If a brick weighs one pound and half a brick, how much does a brick weigh ?

(2) If six hens lay six eggs in six days, how many eggs will twelve hens lay in twelve days ?

(3) Which would you rather have : half a ton of sovereigns or a ton of half-sovereigns ?

(4) Which weighs most—a ton of feathers or a ton of lead ?

(5) Mr. Swindel goes to the Bootmaker, and buys a pair of boots worth 16*s*. He has only a five-pound note, which he gives to the Bootmaker. The Bootmaker, unable to change it, runs across to his friend the Butcher, who gives him five one-pound notes for it. The Bootmaker returns, and gives Mr. Swindel four pounds four shillings change, and Mr. Swindel goes off.

Five minutes later, the Butcher comes across to say the note was bad, so the Bootmaker goes across to his bank and obtains a five-pound note, which he gives to the Butcher.

How much has the Bootmaker lost ?

Did you hear the disgraceful thing that happened at the Exhibition ?

There is a Crêche where they are supposed to look after the babies while the parents enjoy themselves. Last evening a woman got there late, and they gave her a *black* baby and also entirely refused to change.

How disgraceful—how awful !

Well, it's not quite so bad as it seems—you see the woman herself was coal-black.

A very well dressed man met a blind beggar wearing a shabby tweed cap.

The blind beggar said, " Do not turn away—*your* sister was *my* aunt's niece."

What relation are they to each other ?

Answer : Brother and sister.

(The blind beggar was a woman—she had to wear a tweed cap, as it was the only one she had.)

The Puzzle which is said to have Puzzled Einstein

(*Answers on page* 151)

Two horses are twenty miles apart: they start running towards one another at a speed of ten miles per hour. A fly starts from the nose of one as it starts—flies to the nose of the other one, backwards and forwards, until they meet. The fly is flying at the speed of fifteen miles an hour.

How far has it flown when it is crushed between their noses?

For the Muddle-Headed

(1) A. shakes up eight matches in his hands, and then opens them and says: " How many matches have I here? "

B. (counting carefully). " Eight."

A. " No, I'm sure I have seven; look again."

B. " Eight."

A. (patter). " I believe I'm right, but I'll try again." (Shakes again.) " Now how many? "

B. " Eight."

A. " I still think there are seven. Will you give me a penny if I'm wrong? "

B. " Yes."

A. " Well, give me a penny, because I *am* wrong."

(2) Two people start from point A to run to point B. X gets to B in three minutes and back to A in two minutes.

Y gets to B in two minutes and back to A in three minutes. Which gets back to A first?

For the High-brows Only

(*Answers on page* 151)

(1) Write down the Devil's Telephone Number.

(2) Write London without joining the L to the O, and without taking your pencil off the paper.

(3) To improve your writing: Write down Numbers one to nine, excluding the figure eight. Multiply by the figure you write worst.

Then multiply this result by nine—and after this practice we shall hope to see a marked improvement in the figure you write worst.

(4) Turn this into a rhymed couplet without altering the order of the words:—*There was an old lady and she was as deaf as a post.*

A Little Care is Required Here

Suppose you play this game in the year 1932, you must write down 3864, and put it away elaborately under a book.

Note—

If you play this in			1933,	write down		3866.
"	"	"	1934,	"	"	3868.
"	"	"	1935,	"	"	3870.

Then you ask A to write down the year of his marriage, the year of his birth, the number of years he has been married, and finally his age this year. He must then add them all together, and you then turn up the figures you wrote under the book.

Easy Money

(*Answers on page* 151)

(1) A man takes £2 15*s*. 0*d*. to pay four wages.

He pays first,	£1	0	0	which leaves	£1	15	0
He pays another,	1	0	0	which leaves		15	0
Then,		9	0	which leaves		6	0
Then the last,		6	0	which leaves			0
Total	£2	15	0	Total	£2	16	0

Query : Where is the odd 1*s*. ?

(2) A Bank Manager went to the Bank one morning, and on his arrival the Night Watchman said earnestly : " I beg

you will not return home by the 6.20 train as is your usual habit. Last night I dreamed vividly the train was wrecked, and you were killed."

WHAT DID THE BANK MANAGER DO ?

Menus for the Christmas Week-End

"Darling we really must stop the gardener smoking"

Those Were the Days

KING ARTHUR'S CHRISTMAS

They served up salmon, venison and wild boars
By hundreds and by dozens and by scores;
Hogsheads of honey, kilderkins of mustard,
Muttons, and fatted beeves, and bacon swine;
Herons and bitterns, peacocks, swan and bustard,
Teal, mallard, pigeons, widgeons, and in fine,
Plum puddings, pancakes, apple-pies and custard,
And therewithal they drank good Gascon wine,
With mead, and ale and cider of our own,
For porter, punch and negus were not known.

WHISTLECRAFT.

Christmas Week-End

Friday.

LUNCH

* Scrambled Eggs, with asparagus tips in little cases.
Grilled Cutlets—Petit Pois—Potatoes Sauté.
Meringue of Apple.

DINNER

Hare Soup.
Boiled Mackerel.
Fillet of Beef.
Cheese Fritters.
Coffee.

Saturday.

LUNCH

* Baked Smelts.
Spanish Chicken.
Chocolate Mousse.

DINNER

Watercress Soup.
Roast Saddle of Mutton.
Marrons de luxe.
Crême of Haddock on Toast.

* May be omitted if two-course luncheons are more convenient.

Christmas Week-End

Sunday.

LUNCH

* Curried Prawns.
Roast Pheasant.
Compôte of Oranges.

SUPPER

Crême of Chicken Soup.
Cold Saddle Mutton (Salad of Beetroot, Banana and Cream with Walnuts.)
Cold Tongue.
Passion-fruit en coupe.
Coffee.

CHRISTMAS DAY

Monday.

LUNCH

Celery Soup.
Roast Turkey.
Plum Pudding. Mince Pies.
Dessert.

DINNER

Tomato Soup.
Sole à la Cobert.
Canard Sauvage à la Norvégienne.
Pouding glacé à la Noël.
Pâté de foie gras.

* May be omitted if two-course luncheons are more convenient.

Boxing Day

Tuesday.

See page 119; but failing that, here is a fool-proof luncheon for the inexperienced cook:

Lunch

Poached Eggs on Sweet Corn.
Large Dish with thin slices of Galantine,
Tongue, Ham and Cold Turkey.
A Good Salad.
Thinnest Water Biscuits served with Cream Cheese.
Bar-le-duc White Currant Jam and freshly rolled
Butter.
White Wine and Orangeade. Coffee and Cigarettes.

Supper

Clear Soup (out of a bottle).
Tongue or Ham. Lancashire Chicken.
Fruit Salad.

Wednesday.

Lunch

Cauliflower Soufflé.
Salmi of Duck with Olives.
Orange Sauce.
Lemon Sponge.

Visitors depart after lunch.

For the rest of the week, the family must be fed on pink iced cakes, ham in every shape and form, and odds and ends of Christmas fare. If they should, any of them, get invitations to stay away, they *must* be encouraged to accept.

Boxing Day

WORTH A GUINEA A PAGE

Will you try to persuade your guests, for the sake of their complexions, digestions and tempers, to try the effect of a Fruit and Salad day, in order to undo the ill effects of over-eating the day before.

Note.—As the servants usually all go out on Boxing Day, this is a particularly easy form of cooking for the one left at home. I will guarantee that no one will feel hungry if they will try this Menu.

MENU

7.30 *a.m.*

A glass of hot lemon and water on waking, instead of morning tea.

Breakfast.

Three Oranges and half a Grape-fruit.

Luncheon.

A small separate salad for each, made of lettuce, water-cress, finely-shredded radish, raw carrot, onion, celery, mixed lavishly with oil and lemon (not vinegar).

A small dish of ground-nuts and grated cheese for each person which they add at their pleasure.

Apricot Fool served in Grape-fruit glasses.

Afternoon Tea.

A cup of weak China Tea and brown bread and honey.

Dinner.

Four Tomatoes each, mixed with oil and lemon.

Fresh Pineapple. Grapes. Dried Figs and Dates.

Finally.

An early Bed, with a hot lemon drink.

Another Meatless Day

Breakfast.

Coffee. Omelette aux fines herbes.

Luncheon.

Fried Plaice. Sauce Tartare.
Celery Soufflé.

Dinner.

Spinach Soup.
Tomatoes stuffed with sweet corn.
Melted Cheese.

Suppose —

Suppose Mr. Wolf is only two doors off, and you can't afford a turkey, and you can't afford a goose, and you can't even afford a chicken, then you must content yourself with this Christmas Dinner :

MENU

Artichoke Soup.
Sausages—Chestnut purée—Bread Sauce—
Brussel Sprouts—Mashed Potatoes
and Forcemeat Balls.
Christmas Pudding.
Tangerines and Almonds and Raisins and Crackers.

Christmas Lunch in the Tropics

(As it is.)

Tinned Turkey.
Tinned Beans.
Messy Christmas Pudding.
Stale Mince Pies.
Whisky-and-Soda.

(Apoplectic Fit.)

(As it ought to be.)

Cold Chicken masked with white sauce.
Tongue.
Miniature Christmas Puddings with rum poured over, and set alight.
Fruit Salad.
Iced Cider Cup.

Christmas Cookery

An Empire Christmas Pudding

(With accompanying SAUCES, according to recipes supplied by the King's Chef, MR. CEDARD, with Their Majesties' gracious consent.)

1 lb. of Currants—Australia.
1 lb. of Sultanas—Australia or South Africa.
1 lb. of stoned Raisins—Australia or South Africa.
5 ozs. of Minced Apple—United Kingdom or Canada.
1 lb. of Breadcrumbs—United Kingdom.
1 lb. of Beef Suet—United Kingdom.
6½ ozs. of cut Candied Peel—South Africa.
8 ozs. of Flour—United Kingdom.
8 ozs. of Demerara Sugar—British West Indies or British Guiana.
5 eggs—United Kingdom or Irish Free State.
½ oz. Ground Cinnamon—India or Ceylon.
¼ oz. Ground Cloves—Zanzibar.
¼ oz. Ground Nutmegs—British West Indies.
¼ teaspoonful Pudding Spice—India or British West Indies.
* ¼ gill Brandy—Australia, South Africa, Cyprus or Palestine.
* ½ gill Rum—Jamaica or British Guiana.
* 1 pint Old Beer—England, Wales, Scotland or Ireland.

* These ingredients may be regarded as optional provided some other liquid such as milk is substituted—in which case, however, the pudding will lose its keeping qualities.

SAUCE SABAYON

Put into a whipping bowl the yolks of 2 eggs, ¼ oz. castor sugar, ¼ gill South African white wine, ¼ gill water. Set bowl over a slow gas. Whip continuously until quite frothy as whipped cream. Serve immediately. Before serving, a few drops of Cyprus brandy or Jamaica rum may be sprinkled over.

Empire Mince Pies

(According to recipes supplied by the King's Chef, MR. CEDARD, with Their Majesties' gracious consent.)

Prepare puff-paste from the following:—1 lb. flour (United Kingdom), 1 lb. butter (United Kingdom, Australia, New Zealand or Irish Free State), giving six turns. Line mince-pie tins with the paste and fill with the following previously prepared mincemeat:—6 lbs. currants (Australia), 6 lbs. sultanas (Australia), 6 lbs. stoned raisins (South Africa), 4 lbs. chopped mixed peel (South Africa), 4 lbs. Demerara sugar (British West Indies or British Guiana), 1½ ozs. ground cinnamon (India), 1½ ozs. ground nutmegs (British West Indies), 1 oz. ground cloves (Zanzibar), ½ bushel minced russet apples (United Kingdom or Canada), juice of 10 lemons (South Africa), juice of 10 oranges (Palestine or British West Indies), chopped rind of 5 lemons and 5 oranges (Palestine or British West Indies), 1 pint brandy (Australia, South Africa, Cyprus or Palestine), 1 pint rum (South Africa, Jamaica or British Guiana), 1 pint white wine (South Africa), 7 lbs. chopped suet (United Kingdom).

Cover the pies with another layer of paste, wash with egg, and bake in a fairly hot oven. When almost ready, dust with icing sugar and replace in oven until glazed.

The quantities given above will make about 3 dozen pie cases and 40 lbs. of mincemeat. Store in tightly sealed jars.

(A simple and more economical recipe.)

2 lbs. apples (United Kingdom or Canada), 1 lb. grapes (United Kingdom), 1 lb. raisins (South Africa), 1 lb. currants (Australia), ½ lb. Demerara sugar (British West Indies or British Guiana), ½ lb. chopped orange peel (South Africa), rind and juice of 1 lemon and 1 orange (Palestine or British West Indies), 2 ozs. mixed spice (India, British West Indies and Zanzibar), pinch of salt (United Kingdom). When all ingredients are well chopped and mixed, put into jars and tie down at once.

A Rich Christmas Pudding

½ lb. Beef Suet.
2 ozs. Flour.
½ lb. Raisins.
¼ lb. Mixed Peel.
Half a grated Nutmeg.
½ oz. Ground Cinnamon.
1 gill Milk.
½ oz. Mixed Spice.
1 wineglassful of Rum or Brandy.
½ lb. Breadcrumbs.
¼ lb. Sultanas.
¼ lb. Currants.
1 Lemon.
2 ozs. Shredded Almonds.
A pinch of Salt.
4 Eggs.

Skin the suet and chop finely. Clean the fruit, stone the raisins, finely shred the mixed peel, peel and chop the lemon rind. Put all dry ingredients into a basin, and stir well. Add the milk, stir in the eggs one at a time, add the brandy and the strained juice of the lemon. Work the whole thoroughly for some minutes, so that the ingredients are well blended. Put the mixture in a well-greased basin. Boil for about 4 hours. Enough for 9 persons.

SAUCE FOR CHRISTMAS PUDDING

Beat to a light cream equal quantities of butter and castor sugar, flavour with a squeeze of lemon juice, and a teaspoonful of brandy (1 teaspoonful to 2 oz. of butter and 2 oz. sugar). Set on ice until needed, and serve in a glass dish with Plum Pudding.

Inexpensive Christmas Pudding

4 ozs. chopped Suet
,, Flour.
,, Currants.
4 ozs. Raisins.
Breadcrumbs.
2 tablespoonfuls Treacle.
1 teaspoonful Mixed Spice.

Method.—Mix together, moisten with half a pint of milk. Put into greased basin—boil for 8 hours.

Rich Christmas Cake

11 ozs. Butter.
10 ozs. Castor Sugar.
1 lb. Currants.
¼ lb. Mixed Candied Peel.
11 ozs. Flour.
1 lb. Raisins.
¼ lb. Almonds.
6 Eggs.
½ oz. Mixed Spice.
1 wineglassful of Brandy.

Blanch and slice the almonds finely. Stone and chop raisins; shred peel finely. Beat the butter to a cream, add the sugar, then the eggs, well beaten, alternately with the flour; beat all well, and then add the remainder of the ingredients in small quantities. Mix well and turn into a tin lined with greased paper, and bake in a *moderate* oven 3½ to 4 hours or more according to the heat of the oven.

The cake is much improved by keeping 8–12 weeks before using. The mixture can be made into two cakes, and iced before using. They will keep for months iced.

Mrs. Beeton Roasts the Turkey

1 Turkey.
1–2 lbs. Sausage-meat.
1 lb. Forcemeat.
2 Slices of Bacon.
1 pint good Gravy.
Bread Sauce.
Fat for basting.

Method.—Prepare and truss the turkey. Fill the crop with sausage-meat and put veal forcemeat inside the body of the bird. Skewer the bacon over the breast, baste well with hot fat and roast in a moderate oven from 1¾ to 2¼ hours according to age and size of the bird. Baste frequently, and 20 minutes before serving remove the bacon to allow the breast to brown. Remove the trussing strings, serve on a hot dish and send the gravy and bread sauce to table in sauce-boats.

STUFFING FOR TURKEY

Put 1 lb. sausage-meat into a deep bowl with a little grated nutmeg.

Add to this one shredded onion which has been cooked for a few minutes in butter.

Add one egg well beaten.

Have ready about 1 lb. of chestnuts which have been cooked in some good stock.

Mix with stuffing and chestnuts, and stuff the turkey.

CHESTNUT PURÉE

Peel as many roasted chestnuts as are required, and warm them in butter. Moisten with stock and white wine, and simmer over a slow fire until soft. Pound in a mortar, pass through a tammy, and serve very hot.

Those Little Extras

BREAD SAUCE.

1 gill Breadcrumbs.	4 Peppercorns.
½ pint Milk.	½ oz. Butter.
1 small Onion.	Salt.

2 Cloves.

Method.—Put milk into a saucepan, and when it boils, add onion, peppercorns and cloves. Let this stand on the hob 15 minutes covered; strain, add breadcrumbs—stir in the butter and add salt to season. Re-heat and serve.

CHESTNUT FORCEMEAT. Moderate oven. Time—30 minutes.

24 Chestnuts.	Salt.
1 oz. Margarine.	Pepper.
1 oz. Chopped Parsley.	Pinch of Nutmeg.

Method.—Make an incision in the rind of the chestnuts. Put them into a saucepan of boiling water, and boil until tender, say 30 minutes. Remove both outer and inner rind of nuts, and pound the insides in a mortar with margarine. Add the parsley and seasoning, and pound all well together; then use the result for stuffing the turkey.

SAGE AND ONION STUFFING. Moderate oven. Time—25 minutes.

4 Onions.	6 Sage leaves.
4 ozs. Breadcrumbs.	Pepper.
½ oz. Margarine.	Salt.

Method.—Peel onions. Put them into cold water. Bring them to the boil and let them boil for 3 minutes. Add sage leaves, and let them boil 2 minutes longer. Strain and chop onions and sage finely, and return result to the pan with margarine, breadcrumbs and seasoning. Simmer gently, stirring often, for 20 minutes. It is then ready for use.

Those Little Extras

POTATO BALLS.

About 1 lb. Mashed Potatoes. Egg and Breadcrumbs.
Salt and Pepper to taste. Dripping.

Method.—Boil and mash potatoes, add pepper and salt. Roll potatoes into small balls, cover with beaten egg and breadcrumbs, and fry in hot dripping. Drain before use.

BRUSSELS SPROUTS.

Cut off outside leaves of sprouts, wash them in cold water, and blanch them in boiling water for 5 minutes. Drain and finish cooking them in fresh boiling salted water for about 15 minutes. Drain thoroughly.

The Gentle Art of Carving the Turkey

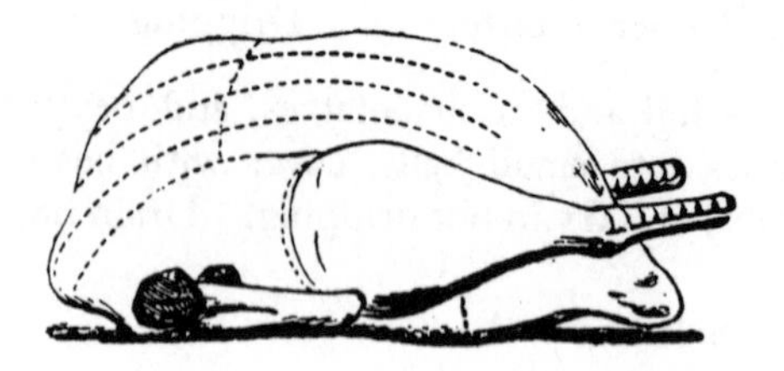

A sharp knife is half the battle.

The breast of a turkey is so large that slices taken neatly from it and from the wings generally suffice for all. The slices should be taken from each side alternately, beginning close to the wings.

Don't forget to add a small portion of forcemeat, chestnut stuffing and half a sausage to each helping.

When it is necessary for the legs to be used they should be separated from the body with a sharp knife and cut in slices.

Believe it or not.—Turkeys were introduced into Europe in the sixteenth century by one of Sebastian Cabot's lieutenants.

ARTICHOKE SOUP

Boil 3 lbs. of Jerusalem Artichokes, which have been peeled, and put for a few minutes in cold water, in a quart of milk, adding to it a teacupful of water. When Artichokes are very soft, rub them through a sieve—flavour with pepper and salt just before serving (when the soup is hot but not boiling), stir in a spoonful or two of cream, and serve with bread cut in dice and fried.

ROAST GOOSE

1 Goose.
Onion Stuffing.
Fat for basting.
¾ pint of good Beef Stock or Gravy.
Apple Sauce.

Method.—Prepare and truss the goose (the poulterer will do this for a small fee), put the onion forcemeat inside the body; baste it well with hot fat, and roast or bake for 2 to 2½ hours, according to size. Baste frequently, and if the surface is not well browned, dredge with flour when the bird is three-quarters cooked. Remove the trussing string, serve on a hot dish, and send the gravy and apple sauce to table in sauce-boats.

APPLE SAUCE

1 lb. Apples.
1½ ozs. Sugar.
1 oz. Butter.
A little water.

Method.—Peel, core and slice apples; put them in stew-pan with sugar, butter and a very little water, and cook until tender.

Time 30–40 minutes. Quantity ½ pint.

For Inexpensive Christmas Pudding, see page 127.

Anything can Happen at Christmas Time

Let us suppose you run out of bread, and the baker is not due until 10 a.m.

Here is a recipe for little loaves made in seven minutes :

SHERWOOD SCONES

A cupful of ordinary flour.
A good teaspoonful of baking powder.
Salt to taste.
Butter the size of a walnut.

Mix with a little milk (sour milk makes them lighter). Roll the dough into strips and plait.

Hot oven, 5–7 minutes.

S.O.S.

If friends should arrive unexpectedly to luncheon when you have nothing but mutton hash, you must throw in a large quantity of Sauce Escoffier Robert, and two handfuls of glacé cherries—and if *that* doesn't delight and dazzle them, they are a poor-spirited lot.

Marrons Glacées

Boil chestnuts in water until they are soft, peeling carefully to avoid breaking them, and dropping at once into cold water to harden them. Drop them carefully in a syrup of sugar cooked to the consistency of glue, and leave them until next day. The syrup strained off the nuts is then poured once more over the chestnuts, which are left to soak overnight, this process being repeated four times, while on the last occasion the sugar is boiled a little longer.

To glacé them, they should be dipped in a fresh syrup made very thick and rich, the chestnuts finally drying on a waxed sheet.

Question.—Isn't it better to buy them?

Fudge

A Way we Have in the School Room

2 lbs. Granulated Sugar.
2 ozs. Margarine.
A little Milk.
1 tin Nestle's Unsweetened Milk.

Put sugar and margarine into a large saucepan and just " grey " the sugar with a little milk (not too much—the more you put the longer it takes to boil).

Let it boil for 10 minutes and then pour in the condensed milk (stirring hard or it burns).

Stir for 20–40 minutes (it seems to vary). To see whether it is done, drop a very little into a saucer of cold water, roll it into a ball and drop it on to the table. When it makes a " pingy " noise it is done (and if it won't roll into a ball it means the fudge isn't nearly ready).

Take it off the fire, let it cool for 10 minutes and then beat it until it stiffens a little, and pour it out on to grease-proof paper.

The chief difficulty is to induce it to set, and we generally end by eating ours out of the spoon, which is just as nice and simply means it hasn't been cooked for quite long enough. When cool, cut it into squares with a knife.

(Recipe kindly supplied by the Champion Fudge-maker of England's most famous girls' school.)

Once Met Never Forgotten

RECIPES FOR PREPARING RUSSIAN BLENIE

No. 1.

2 ozs. Buckwheat Flour.
1 teaspoonful Yeast.
½ glass Warm Milk.
1 tablespoonful Castor Sugar.
2 Yolks Eggs.
1 oz. Melted Butter.
Pinch of Salt.
1¼ pt. Fresh Cream.
2 Whites Eggs.

Mix yeast and warm milk together, gradually adding flour, then keep in warm place until it rises. Then mix the yolks of the two eggs with the sugar and melted butter, and add a pinch of salt—mix these two mixtures together, put in a warm place for one hour until it rises for the second time. Afterwards, whisk the whites of the eggs and gradually add it to the paste, and after that also add ¼ pt. cream. Fry gently in butter in small portions at a time, dropping small quantities of butter on the Blenie. Fry it until it becomes a golden colour and then turn it over, place on a very hot plate and serve it hot with Caviare Orelle, fresh sour cream and tablespoonful of melted butter.

RUSSIAN FRESH SOUR CREAM SPECIALLY FOR BLENIE

No. 2.

Mix three or four drops lemon juice in a ¼ pt. fresh cream and whip until thick. It must be made four or five hours before serving.

Hang the Expense!

(Mother Hubbard is out of this scene.)

Caviare.
Truffles du Perigord.
Bar-le-duc White Currant Jam.
Foie gras.
Romany Biscuits.
Real Turtle Soup.
Bêche de Mer Soup.
Olives stuffed with Sweet Pepper.
Quails farcies in Aspic.
Boar's Head.
A Bradenham Ham.
Bath Olivers.
Celery Wafers.
Brittsalts.
Tiptree's Damson Cheese.
Cherries in Maraschino.
Smoked Salmon.
Pimentos.
Prawns.
Pine Kernels.
Small Mushrooms.

The Emergency Store Cupboard

Tins :

Libby's Pressed Beef.
Jackson's Julienne Soup.
Heinz' Cream of Tomato Soup.

Ideal Milk.
Sweet Corn.
Tongue.
Salmon.
Lobster.

Raspberries.
Prepared Grape-fruit.
Loganberries.
Passion-fruit.

Tablets of :

Ivelcon Soup (add a dash of Worcester Sauce).
Bifti Tomato Soup.
Puffed Rice.
Black Treacle.

Macaroni.
Marmite.

Sardines.
Concentrated Egg Mixture.
Sauce Escoffier Diable and Robert.
Ready-made Puff Pastry.
Sponge Fingers.

" The Uninvited Guest is sent by God."

Old Irish Saying.

That Dear Old Ham

One of the problems that confronts the Hostess is what to do with that dear old ham Uncle George sends every year. It has appeared on the sideboard at many breakfasts, and as many luncheons ; it has been warmed up with champagne sauce ; it has been made into a mousse ; it has been heated up with mustard and eaten as a savoury. It has formed a pretty packet of sandwiches for a departing guest, and it has helped stuff a vol-au-vent. But still it stares you in the face every time you go to the larder.

There is clearly only one thing to be done with it. . . . Pack it up neatly, and send it to the Little Sisters of the Poor, who will be delighted to feed their old folks on such a delicacy.

The Wassail Bowl

Come, butler, come bring us a bowl of your best,
And we hope your soul in Heaven shall rest ;
But if you do bring us a bowl of your small,
Then down shall go butler, the bowl and all.

The Wassail Bowl

Put into a bowl half a pound of Lisbon or Barbadoes sugar; pour on it one pint of warm beer; grate a nutmeg and some ginger into it; add four glasses of sherry and five additional pints of beer; stir it well; sweeten it to your taste; let it stand covered up two or three hours, then put in three or four roasted crab-apples, and it is fit for use. A couple or three slices of lemon, and a few lumps of loaf sugar rubbed on the peel of a lemon are introduced.

Bottle this mixture, and in a few days it may be drank in a state of effervescence.

LEANDER PUNCH

(So called after the Club of that name.)

Four glasses of whisky (Irish if possible), two glasses of brandy, and the juice and peel of one large lemon. Add boiling water to make a quart, and if not enough, *ad libitum*. Then boil a wine-glass of good old ale, and put the froth into the punch with one tablespoonful of the ale; sweeten to the taste and stir it. If it stands in a jug near the fire for half an hour it will be improved.

CHAMPAGNE CUP

1 bot. Champagne (cheap).
1 liqueur of Brandy.
1 liqueur of Maraschino.
1 liqueur of Curaçoa.
1 bot. Soda.
Ice.

Liqueurs can be added a little, if desired.

HOT TODDY

To three-quarters of a pint of boiling water add half a pint of brandy, half a pint of whisky, the juice of three lemons and one lemon thinly sliced, quarter of a pound of sugar, half a teaspoonful of ginger essence and half a teaspoonful of mixed spice. Stir the mixture well and heat till it is nearly boiling.

Hot Toddy should be served *hot*, and is a most grateful nightcap on cold winter evenings.

OXFORD PUNCH

Extract the juice from the rind of three lemons, by rubbing loaf sugar on them. The peel of two Seville oranges and two lemons, cut extremely thin. The juice of four Seville oranges and ten lemons. Six glasses of calves-feet jelly in a liquid state. The above to be put into a jug, and stirred well together. Pour two quarts of boiling water on the mixture, cover the jug closely, and place it near the fire for a quarter of an hour. Then strain the liquid through a sieve into a punch bowl or jug, sweeten it with a bottle of capillaire, and add half a pint of white wine, a pint of French brandy, a pint of Jamaica rum, and a bottle of orange shrub; the mixture to be stirred as the spirits are poured in. If not sufficiently sweet add loaf sugar gradually in small quantities, or a spoonful or two of capillaire.

PUNCH À LA ROMAINE

(For 12 people.)

1 bot. Champagne.
½ bot. Rum.
2 liq. glasses Liq. Brandy.
2 ,, ,, Benedictine.
2 ,, ,, Curaçoa.
2 ,, ,, Tangerino.
2 ,, ,, Cherry Brandy.
1 grated Nutmeg.
1 small bot. Essence of Lime.
½ lb. Sugar (moist).
½ lb. Cream.
1 bot. Soda-water.
10 lbs. Ice.

MULLED CLARET

1 pint Claret.
½ pint Boiling Water.
Sugar, Nutmeg and Cinnamon to taste.

Heat the claret nearly to boiling point; add the boiling water, sugar, nutmeg and cinnamon to taste, and serve hot.

Envoi

Now grocers trade
Is in request
For plums and spices
Of the best.

Good cheer doth with
This month agree
And dainty chaks
Must sweetned be.

Mirth and gladness
Doth abound
And strong beer in
Each house is found.

Minc'd Pies, roast Beef
With other cheer
And feasting doth
Conclude the year.

POOR ROBIN, 1677.

Christmas Catering Lists

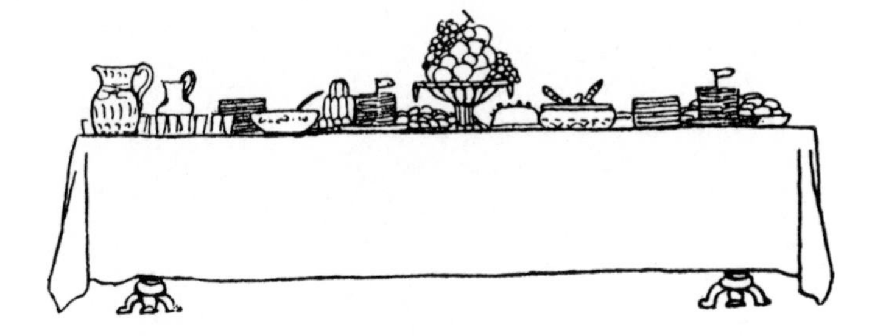

Cold Supper for an All-night Dance

One Hundred Guests.

20 Lobsters for Mayonnaise.
50 Foie Gras Croûtes.
50 Oyster and Veal Patties.
1 Glazed and Decorated Ham.
1 Young Roast Turkey.
6 lbs. Glazed Pressed Beef.
2 Galantines of Chicken.
10 French Salads, to make six portions each.
10 Tomato and Lettuce Salads, to make six portions each.
150 French Pastries.
50 Meringues and Cream.
50 Pêches Melba.
50 Small Individual Macedoines of Fruit.
8 Bowls of Fruit Salad, to make ten portions.
30 Quarts of Champagne (and Cider) Cup.
200 Ice Creams.
12 Quarts Coffee.
30 Quarts Lemonade and Orangeade.

Light Refreshments at a Dance for One Hundred Guests

300 Small Sandwiches.	75 Lobster Patties.
75 Small Sausage Rolls.	100 Small Iced Cakes.
150 Ices: peach, tangerine, chocolate.	
6 lbs. Cakes of various kinds.	20 Quarts Hock Cup.
16 Quarts Lemonade.	10 Quarts Cider Cup.
16 Quarts Orangeade.	8 Quarts Coffee.

16 Quarts of Soup served on departure.

The Buffet Supper for a Small Party

Lobster Patties. Small Sausage Rolls. Tongue and Foie-Gras Sandwiches. Nut and Cream Sandwiches. Fruit Salad. Iced Cakes. Plumcake. Rolled Brown and White Bread-and-butter. Orangeade. Lemonade. Cider Cup. Hot Coffee.

To save labour, make all sandwiches from small bridge rolls. Buy ready-made puff pastry for the lobster patties.

Nut and Cream Sandwiches.—Made with brown bread and butter. Use 2 ozs. walnuts to 6*d.* packet of cream cheese (= 20 sandwiches). Chop walnuts finely and mix with cream cheese, seasoning well with pepper and salt.

Cider Cup.—Take two large bottles of cider and soda-water to make up the quantity desired. Add a little pine-apple (tinned), orange, a few stoned grapes, slices of apple and cucumber peel. A little gin is an improvement. Put into the refrigerator, or pack round with ice.

Odds and Ends

SCHOOL TREAT FOR FORTY CHILDREN

50 Buns.	2 lbs. Jam.
3 lbs. Biscuits.	3 lbs. Sugar.
4 Loaves.	¾ lb. Tea.
2 lbs. Butter.	5 pints Milk.

COFFEE AND BISCUITS FOR ONE HUNDRED AT A MOTHERS' MEETING

1¼ lbs. Coffee.	4 lbs. Sugar.
2 gallons Milk.	12 lbs. Mixed Biscuits

FIFTY FRIENDS COME TO TEA

1. One pound of tea makes 200 small tea-cups.
2. One pound of coffee provides 96 coffee-cups or 48 tea-cups of coffee.
3. Three pounds of loaf sugar should be allowed for 50 people.
4. It is possible to cut 50 slices of bread from a quartern loaf.
5. Three quarts of milk should be allowed for tea for 50 people.
6. Four quarts of milk serve for coffee for 50 people.
7. One pound of butter should be provided when cutting bread and butter for 50 people.

AT A TEA-PARTY

Roughly speaking, each guest will eat :

2 Sandwiches.
1 Slice of Bread-and-butter.
1 Slice of Cake, and
1 Scone.

A pint of ice-cream is sufficient for ten portions (but this does not apply to schoolboys).

Recipes

WATERCRESS SOUP

2 cups of good White Stock.
2 bunches Watercress.
3 tablespoonfuls Butter.
2 tablespoonfuls Flour.
½ a cup of milk.
1 yolk of Egg.
Salt and Pepper.

Cut finely leaves of watercress. Cook for five minutes in two tablespoonfuls of butter, add stock and boil for five minutes. Thicken with butter and flour cooked together, add salt and pepper. Just before serving, add milk and egg yolk slightly beaten.

LANCASHIRE CHICKEN

Boil a chicken (very little water and let it cook in its steam). Take meat off bones, and cut it up fine. Fry some bacon. Arrange meat in alternate layers of chicken and bacon. Add two hard-boiled eggs. Cover all with thick white sauce, and let it stand.

ROAST WILD DUCK IN THE NORWEGIAN MANNER

Roast a couple of wild ducks. Cut the breast in slices and replace the meat so that the guests can help themselves. Serve each bird in a deep entrée dish and cover it with a rich game sauce flavoured with port wine and truffles.

With this dish hand round a compoté of apples and cranberries.

ORANGE COMPOTÉ

Take three unskinned oranges and their weight in sugar. Boil the oranges in three or four clean waters till the skin is quite soft, then make a syrup of the sugar and the last water the oranges were boiled in, and cut the oranges into equal bits, keeping the skin on.

Put the bits into the syrup for a few minutes, and use it when cold. Use plenty of syrup, and hand round orange iced cake.

(*Note.*—An Emperor could be asked to meet this simple dish.)

MARRONS DE LUXE

Put marrons glacées into grape-fruit glasses, pour Maraschino over them, and put whipped cream on top. Serve with " Cats' Tongue " biscuits.

POUDING GLACE À LA NOËL

(In its simplest form.)

Buy vanilla ice block from Lyons. Stick burnt almonds into it, and hand round with it hot thick rich chocolate sauce in a silver sauce-boat.

Answers to Catches, etc.

Page 107.

(1) Two pounds.
(2) Twenty-four.
(3) A ton of half sovereigns.
(4) They weigh the same.
(5) The pair of boots and four pounds four shillings.

Page 109.

15 miles.
(2) Whichever started first.

Page 110.

(1) 77¾ (turn this upside down).

(2) 

(4) There was an old lady and she
Was as deaf as a P. O. S. T.

Page 111.

(2) He sacked the night watchman for being asleep.

AN APOLOGY

Page 21.

" Little things that enliven house-parties."

The friend who performs these entertaining tricks refuses to part with their secret unless he is paid fifty pounds . . . the editor frankly does not think them worth it (especially when you know how simple they are !)

Finis

The Lord of Misrule is no mean man for his time, and the guests of the high table must lack no wine : the lusty bloods must look about them like men, and piping and dancing puts away much melancholy : stolen venison is sweet and a fat coney is worth money : pitfalls are now set for small birds, and a woodcock hangs himself in a gin : a good fire heats all the house, and a full alms-basket makes the beggars' prayers —the maskers and the mummers make merry sport, but if they lose their money their drum goes dead : swearers and swaggerers are sent away to the ale-house, and unruly wenches go in danger of judgment : musicians now make their instruments speak out and a good song is worth the hearing. In sum, it is a holy time, a duty in Christians for the remembrance of Christ and custom among friends for the maintenance of good-fellowship. In brief I thus conclude it : I hold it a memory of the Heaven's love and the world's peace, the mirth of the honest and the meeting of the friendly.

Farewell.

NICHOLAS BRETON, 1626.